D0562933

TELEVISION AND IRISH SOCIETY

21 Years of Irish Television

edited by
MARTIN McLOONE
Education Officer, Irish Film Institute
and
JOHN MacMAHON
Education Programmes Officer, Radio Telefís Éireann

an RTE/IFI publication
1984

Published 1984 by
Radio Telefís Éireann, Dublin 4, Ireland

Copyright © 1984 by Irish Film Institute

ISBN 0-86029-001-8

Typeset in 10 pt. Times Roman and printed by
P.A.C., 147 Lr. Drumcondra Rd., Dublin 9.

Contents

Notes on Contributors

Martin McLoone is Education Officer, Irish Film Institute, and Secretary of the Media Association of Ireland.

T. V. Finn is Deputy Director-General, Radio Telefís Éireann.

Luke Gibbons is a lecturer in Communications at the National Institute for Higher Education (Dublin) and a Council Member of the Irish Film Institute.

Mary Kelly is Lecturer in Sociology at University College, Dublin, and Treasurer of the Media Association of Ireland.

Maurice Earls is a bookseller and is completing a Ph.D. thesis on 'The Politics of the Dublin Press, 1815-1850' at University College, Dublin.

Barbara O'Connor is a postgraduate research student in sociology at University College, Dublin, specialising in the field of women and television drama.

Kevin Rockett is a film critic and historian, and a Council Member of the Irish Film Institute and the Media Association of Ireland.

Introduction

Martin McLoone

These essays were first read as papers at the Irish Film Institute Summer School 1983, *Television And Society – 21 Years Of Irish Television*. Since then, they have been revised and updated and are presented here as the first major contributions to an area of study sadly neglected or badly misrepresented until now. As such, it is perhaps useful to put the essays into context. Firstly, since none of the essays deals specifically with the historical development of RTE, nor its institutional structures, it is necessary to sketch in some of the factors which make Irish public broadcasting what it is today. Secondly, since the approach adopted by the essays is largely different from existing writing about television, it is also necessary to discuss briefly some of the problems facing television studies in Ireland and explain the rationale and methodology adopted here.

1. The Development of Television in Ireland 1961-1984
Irish television was inaugurated on December 31st 1961.[1] The new service emerged after nearly five years of debate and controversy over how it should be structured and financed and what the role of television should or could be in the traditional conservatism of Irish society.

The history and development of Irish television over the last twenty-three years can best be understood by reference to three key factors which have dominated the terms of these debates.

Firstly, Irish society in 1961 was emerging from a period of almost forty years of economic and social conservatism and a relative isolation from mainstream European influences.

Secondly, following directly from this, debates tended to centre on the possible effects that television might have on the social structures of Irish society, especially since large sections of the Irish audience were already receiving "fall-out" signals from British television.

Thirdly, the conservative, sometimes authoritarian, nature of decision making in Ireland tended to give an added charge to debates about public broadcasting and its relationship to the State.

Given this climate into which the new service emerged, the original enabling Act, the Broadcasting Act of 1960, was a surprisingly liberal piece of legislation.[2] In 1961 over 30% of potential television homes were already receiving British television so Irish audiences were familiar with two models of broadcasting, public service broadcasting (BBC) and commercial television (ITV). In effect, the 1960 Act chose the public service model, financed under a mixed economy system.

By the terms of the Act, responsibility for all broadcasting in Ireland was vested in a statutory, independent authority, originally the Radio Éireann Authority and since 1966, the Radio Telefís Éireann Authority (RTE). The model used was that of the BBC and great emphasis was placed on the independence of the Authority from both Government and the Civil Service (which had, in effect, controlled radio broadcasting since 1926).[3]

However, the Act reserved considerable powers to the Minister for Posts and Telegraphs, including the right to appoint or remove from office the members of the Authority and the right to issue directives in regard to broadcast matters.

Throughout the 1960s and into the mid-seventies, RTE enjoyed a stormy relationship with the State. In 1966, for instance, the then Minister of Agriculture, Mr. Charles Haughey, objected to RTE News juxtaposing a statement of his with that of the leader of the Irish Farmers Association during a dispute over government subsidies to farming. The Minister felt that his statement should carry more weight than that of the farmers' leader.

In a subsequent debate in the Dáil the then Taoiseach, Seán Lemass, stated —

> "Radio Telefís Éireann was set up by legislation as an instrument of public policy and as such is responsible to the government. . . . The government reject the view that Radio Telefís Éireann should be, either generally or in regard to its current affairs and news programmes, completely independent of government supervision."[4]

This statement had more in common with the Gaullist model of public broadcasting in France than it had even with the Reithian interpretation of public broadcasting in Britain. Over the next few years, this difference of interpretation over independence continued to cause friction between RTE and Government. In 1967, for example, a government directive stopped an RTE news team from going to North Vietnam and in 1968 from visiting Biafra.

With the outbreak of violence in Northern Ireland in 1968, relations between RTE and Government deteriorated significantly. Finally in 1972, the Minister of the day, Mr. Gerard Collins, sacked the whole RTE Authority over the broadcasting of a report of an interview with a Provisional IRA spokesman.

The Broadcasting (Amendment) Act 1976, inspired by Dr. Conor Cruise O'Brien, attempted to clarify the issue of independence. The Act restricted to some extent the Minister's powers by stipulating that appointments and removals from office must have the assent of both Houses of the Irish Parliament. Under Section 31 of the Act, an order prohibiting interviews with named organisations must receive assent of both Houses and this order is presently in operation (July 1984) in regard to organisations like Sinn Féin, the IRA and the UVF. This order continues to be a matter of controversy, especially with television journalists who feel that their ability to report on issues relating to Northern Ireland is seriously impaired.

Finance

RTE is a public broadcasting service that is financed under a mixed economy system. The Minister collects licence fees on behalf of RTE and is required to forward these to the Authority after deduction of a collecting charge. The Authority is empowered to augment income from licence fees by selling advertising time on radio and television. Originally the revenue from licence fees made up nearly 70% of total income but in the last year for which figures are available (1982) advertising revenue accounted for 60% of total income.

Two reasons are adduced for this. Firstly, the rate of licence evasion is one of the highest in Europe (only Italy compares with Ireland in this regard) and evasion is estimated to have cost RTE IR£8m. in lost revenue in 1983. Secondly the present licence fee of IR£34 for black and white, and IR£52 for colour sets is one of the lowest in Europe and is felt by RTE to be too low. Revenue from licence fees is limited anyway, because of the small population in Ireland, amounting to just over 900,000 television households. (For the spread of television in Ireland and the television "map" today see Appendix Two.)

In 1984, it is estimated that 66% of Irish homes are now receiving good quality signals from British television. This represents considerable competition for RTE and there is evidence that advertising revenue is levelling off as a direct result. Interestingly, these signals from Britain are now being relayed increasingly through cable-systems making the rate of cable penetration in Ireland one of the highest in the world. In Dublin, for example, over 80% of households are now receiving signals through six-channel cable-systems and recent cabling in Cork is reputed to have a twenty-six channel capacity.

In 1984, a subsidiary company of RTE, RTE Relays, accounted for over 80% of Dublin's cabling, a situation that means RTE owns most of the system that brings in its competition from Britain. However, in its twelve year existence, RTE Relays has been a consistently profitable operation and the near monopoly of the system in Dublin means that Irish public broadcasting benefits considerably from largely controlling the influx of signals that otherwise would be in the control of private commercial companies.

Elsewhere in the country, private cable operators must pay a levy of 15% on gross receipts to RTE and in the terms of licence agreements these private companies must carry the two RTE channels as well as the four British channels.

Pirate Radio and Commercial Broadcasting

RTE retains a monopoly on broadcasting in Ireland. However, since the mid-1970s there has been a steady increase in the number of pirate radio stations operating mostly in the cities and larger towns. No effective government action has been taken against the pirates and their increasing efficiency and signal quality has resulted in growing listenership. Already pirate radio is posing considerable competition, especially in Dublin, in regard to advertising revenue.

In early 1984, the Irish government released a discussion document on commercial and community radio and it is expected that commercial radio will be legalised in the near future. At the moment, it would appear that there are no serious proposals for commercial television. In 1981/82, in Dublin, an attempt was made to establish a pirate television service, an off-shoot of one of the pirate radio stations, but this was swiftly and effectively dealt with.

However, it is true to say that Ireland has no clear policy in regard to broadcasting and as yet no serious debate about the future of public broadcasting has taken place. This is very regrettable given the emergence of commercial broadcasting in the near future, the increasing audience in Ireland for British television, the high level of cable penetration with the possibility of greater channel capacity and finally the imminence of direct satellite broadcasting.

RTE has been involved in satellite experiments with the European Broadcasting Union (EBU) and in statements issued in connection with future policy, RTE would seem to favour an agreed European policy for future development. However, the implications of the Hunt Report in Britain for such an agreed policy and the possible effects of the Hunt recommendations on broadcasting in Ireland have never been fully debated.

2. Studying Television in Ireland

> I find television very educational. Every time someone switches it on, I go into another room and read a good book.
>
> Groucho Marx.

Most worthwhile writing on television in Ireland has tended to concentrate on the institutional structures of RTE and on the relationship between RTE and the State. Most other writing has tended to be negative, dismissive or downright hostile. This collection of essays will, hopefully, redress the balance to some extent. In offering analyses of specific programmes and their structures, forms and conventions, it is also hoped that this volume will contribute to the development of the emerging discipline of *television studies,* either as a subject in its own right or as part of more general *media studies* programmes.

It must be admitted, though, that in Ireland, as in many other countries where television has assumed such a dominant cultural position, it is still considered rather perverse to expend intellectual effort on what is perceived as an ephemeral and disposable medium.

The problems facing television studies can be best illustrated by looking briefly at traditional newspaper criticism of the medium. Television has, by and large, played the role of Margaret Dumont to the television critic's Groucho Marx. It is essentially the butt of a "superior" wit, whose real interest in culture is literary.

The person who has laid most claim to the Groucho mantle is Clive James, for many years television critic of the *Observer.* His approach to programmes was wholly impressionistic, using television merely as an excuse to throw out a series of predictable gags and one liners that rarely offered any insights to the medium itself. His column was, in effect, a grand deception, offering uninformed ammunition for the prejudices of those who didn't like television anyway.

Why was James able to get away with this so-called criticism for ten years? Mike Poole offers the following observations.

> *"The answer is simple: it sold newspapers. James's column at its height was said to be worth 10,000 on the* Observer's *circulation. He was employed to be funny and in a sense it just happened that his chosen peg was television. . . . Even so, this still leaves the question of how he actually practised this highly lucrative deception. Again, the answer is relatively straightforward: for all his avowed populism, James wrote about television as if he were indeed writing about something else. And the something else was, of course, our old friend literary culture. When, for instance, he seeks to define the qualities required to deal as a critic with the sheer multifariousness of television's output, James instinctively reaches for Keats' formulation of a 'negative capability', an archetypal Romantic concept some 150 years of age and one nowhere used by Keats himself in relation to the* critical *faculty. James also habitually collapses every narrative, however specifically televisual, back into the realist framework of the 'novelistic'. Thus, despite its elaborate distancing devices and deliberately non-naturalistic use of adult actors to play children, Dennis Potter's* Blue Remembered Hills *is challenged on the crass grounds that it is not 'realistic'."*[5]

Many of the prejudices and approaches to television, evident in Clive James, find echoes in Ireland. For example, it is evident that, with one or two notable exceptions over the years, television (and cinema) critics in Ireland approach their work from an essentially literary tradition, looking for character and plot at the expense of the visual and the generic. There is rarely any engagement with the specific forms of television nor an indication of how these mobilise meaning and viewer responses.

Television is a form of culture, but it is, in essence, different from literary culture. The traditional critical approaches of literary culture must be drastically revised if they are to offer any insights on televisual culture. As John Fiske and John Hartley contend —

> "The tools of literary and dramatic appreciation are by now very sophisticated. But these tools will not necessarily do for television. Just as literature is not the same 'thing' as drama . . . so television differs from both. . . . Hence the tools of traditional literary criticism do not quite fit the television discourse. . . . Any attempt to decode a television 'text' as if it were a literary text is thus not only doomed to failure but is also likely to result in a negative evaluation of the medium, based on its inability to do a job for which it is in fact fundamentally unsuited."[6]

The dominance of a rich literary and dramatic culture reverberates through all areas of the arts and education in Ireland. Not only does it give rise to a dominant form of criticism that is likely to be dismissive of other forms of culture, but it has also harnessed to itself an in-built resistance to educational progress. It is particularly unfortunate that in an age when all the mass media are so demonstrably popular that media studies, and specifically television studies, still have to fight for curriculum acceptance.

However, there is a further complication. Even when television is taken seriously, the totally negative attitudes implicit in literary evaluations can predominate. There are two manifestations of this negativity.

Firstly there is a traditional left approach which sees television as a soporific provided inexpensively from a capitalist society intent on dulling the critical faculties of the mass population and thereby winning acceptance of the status quo. This approach tends to dismiss television as an ideological propaganda mechanism and sees no value in its mass popularity, its diversity of forms and subject matters nor its unrivalled ability to educate and provoke thought across a broad range of issues. Television is a closed system, without contradiction or loose ends and the television audience is perceived as a malleable totality, racing, lemming-like, to its own subjugation.

Secondly, there is a conservative approach which sees television as a dangerously subversive force attacking everything that is human and congealing in society and undermining traditional values and morality. The prime victims of television are seen to be the family and the sexual morality of, especially, the young. This approach to television tends to blame the medium for everything in society that is held to be unwholesome.

Both approaches presume the same total, passive audience and both rely on superficial consideration of what the programmes say or on their underlying structures that contain and make obvious their messages. Both approaches characterise television as a forceful influence on society, though from very different positions. A traditional left approach assumes that television is moulded and structured in total by the economics of its institutional structure so that monopoly capitalist society produces monopoly capitalist television that in return re-inforces monopoly capitalist society. It is a closed circuit of cause and effect. The conservative approach assumes that what appears on the screen, be it sex or violence, is mimicked in society directly and causes everything from child molestation to muggings of pensioners. It is, again, a closed circuit of cause and effect. Finally, both these approaches eschew any cultural consideration of television, assuming that just because it is popular, it cannot, therefore, have any cultural "value". This is the most depressing, and elitist, closed circuit of them all.

These essays, then, challenge dominant literary-based judgements of television and offer correctives to the negativity of traditional assessments of the medium, whether from the left or the right. They are studies that grow out of the new discipline (or more correctly the new cross-disciplinary field) of media studies. Their aim is to offer systematic analyses of television's forms and through reference to specific programmes over two decades of rapid change in Ireland, they also attempt to open out some of the closed circuits that have traditionally dominated thinking about the relation between television and society.

They assume, for example, that television, like all forms of culture, exists in a more dynamic relationship to the socio-economic structures which both produce and then consume its messages. The complexities of this dynamic offer many more opportunities and potentialities for progress than might be traditionally accepted by commentators on the left. The complexities of this dynamic also limit the potential influence of television on social behaviour to a greater extent than commentators on the right have traditionally observed.

For example, in their discussions of popular dramatic forms both Luke Gibbons and Martin McLoone attempt to demonstrate the progressive potential of the series and serial form by close reference to programmes which set out deliberately to raise issues of social concern. Luke Gibbons traces the development of Irish television drama over the last two decades and argues that the "dead-hand" of the Romantic dramatic tradition of the Literary Revival exercised a negative influence on the development of the single television play. It was, ironically, the much despised form of the continuous serial which broke with romantic representations of Irish rural life, offering, almost for the first time in Irish culture, a new realist aesthetic in the form of the long-running serial *The Riordans*. The structures and conventions of the serial allowed it to tap directly into contemporary rural realities and investigate the changing social relationship of the family unit farm and a host of other issues.

Martin McLoone, on the other hand, concentrates on urban-based drama serials and series. In a culture dominated by an ideology of romantic ruralism, the mere presence of the city and the urban working-class on television was an important cultural shift. By tracing the development of this urban discourse leading up to the 1980 production of *Strumpet City,* he argues that television can be seen to offer a particularly liberal or social democratic ideology and in *Strumpet City* especially this discourse potentially offers even more radical critiques of Irish society.

In the third essay on television drama, Barbara O'Connor discusses the way in which women have been represented and how issues of particular concern to women have been raised through a number of RTE productions. Again, she identifies the importance of the serial form as a forum for raising issues and for giving women a more central dramatic role than has traditionally been the case.

In contrast, the other three essays offer analyses of the limitations of television forms, again, ironically, those forms which have traditionally been accused of radical or subversive effects. Mary Kelly traces the development of RTE current affairs, discussing the implications of the rather unhappy relationship between current affairs programmes and the politicians themselves. Like all the essays in this volume, there is particular concern with the formal organisation of the programmes. Far from being the radical, frontier-blazing programmes as they have often been described, Mary Kelly points out how RTE current affairs attempts to mobilise a middle-ground point of view, and she demonstrates this process through analyses of *Today Tonight* reports.

A similar conclusion is arrived at by Maurice Earls in his discussion of *The Late Late Show,* often pilloried by more traditional conservative opinion as a dangerously subversive and immoral programme. In fact, by looking at the controversies it generated, especially in the 1960s, Maurice Earls argues that *The Late Late Show* is essentially a conservative programme, though committed to a more liberal version of society. Through the mediating presence of its host, Gay Byrne, the programme mirrored the changing climate of the country in general, offering, at a popular cultural level, support for the modernising impulses of the economy at large.

The other contributions look to the future, though in very different ways. In the opening paper, Vincent Finn, Deputy Director General of RTE, points out some of the problems facing public broadcasting in Ireland and offers some suggestions for the future structures of television. New technologies and the subsequent changes in television production and consumption are primary concerns for broadcasters today and Vincent Finn gives some insights into how RTE would like to see the future develop. Kevin Rockett is also concerned with future structures of television. However, his concern is with programme forms and contents, arguing that present television practices offer only a limited one-way flow of information and opinion. He locates the problem with present practices within the dual drive of television towards narrativisation on the one hand and a professional remoteness on the other. Together these limit what can be said on television and who can have access to expression. He calls for a greater diversity of form, including non-narrative and more experimental forms as well as a more fully developed concept of "access television" than that which currently operates. (In reviewing his original script Kevin Rockett has been able to take account of RTE "Access — Community Television" screened from November 1983 to April 1984.)

It is hoped that the essays in this volume will contribute to what all the writers see as a great failing in contemporary Irish culture — the relative lack of serious debate or positive assessment of the role of television in culture and society. Finally, it is hoped that the publication of this volume will contribute to the greater acceptance at all levels of education of the need for television studies in Ireland and that it can provide some guidelines for defining what this field of study should be.

REFERENCES

1. For a description of the opening evening of Irish television see Lelia Doolan, Jack Dowling and Bob Quinn, *Sit Down And Be Counted,* (Dublin, Wellington Publishers Ltd., 1969). The book is, by now, a "classic" account of Irish television's first few years. It records the struggles of some producers for independence and details the institutional and commercial pressures which programme makers were subject to.

2. For a detailed discussion of the Broadcasting Act 1960, and subsequent amendments, see Desmond Fisher, *Broadcasting In Ireland,* (London, Routledge and Kegan Paul Ltd., 1978). For a fairly straightforward account of the early history of broadcasting in Ireland, see Maurice Gorham, *Forty Years Of Irish Broadcasting,* (Dublin, Talbot Press, 1967).

3. Gorham, *op. cit.*

4. Quoted in Fisher, *op. cit.*

5. Mike Poole, "The Cult Of The Generalist: British Television Criticism 1936-83" in *Screen,* (Vol. 25, No. 2, Mar./April, 1984).

6. John Fiske and John Hartley, *Reading Television,* (London, Methuen & Co. Ltd., 1978).

1   The Future of Public Service Broadcasting*

T.V. Finn

Twenty-first anniversaries are usually occasions on which the past is reviewed and the future is projected with some clarity and confidence. I feel it would be worthwhile to spend a few minutes on the former part of such an exercise before attempting the second, more important part. In doing so, however, I am conscious of the wisdom of an expert on broadcasting who said that 'if the past is any guide the future is unpredictable'.

One thing can, however, be clearly stated at the outset, because it unifies all our concern about the future of public service broadcasting in this country and is both implicit and explicit in the specialist papers in this volume. That is, the fact that among practitioners and critics, and from the development of technology itself, there is a gradual subversion of the sytem which, I believe, will turn the older monoliths (which are in danger of looking and behaving like worn-out monsters) into more appropriate channels for the age they are to serve. Television studies, of which this volume marks the start in Ireland, will show us both the strengths and the weaknesses of our work. In RTE we need this kind of impartial criticism and to have the culture of a television station analysed as it is here is an invaluable service which we welcome unreservedly.

When radio and television were introduced in Europe, they were for historical reasons generally structured as public service entities. The scarcity of available frequencies and production facilities requiring considerable initial capital outlay led the state authorities to set up organisations and grant them public service licences. The charters or mandate of these organisations behoved them to provide a service which was accessible to all, and a programme schedule which was both tailored

*Based on an address to the Irish Film Institute, 1 July 1983.

to the public's tastes and expectations and included education, information and entertainment as vital components.

Virtually everywhere in Europe, television services have as a result been distributed through a monopoly or oligopoly.

At the same time, governments have tried to ensure stable sources of income for these organisations, thereby enabling them to invest substantial sums in developing their distribution networks and production facilities and to finance a considerable amount of their own material.

Public service broadcasters have therefore been in a position to offer a balanced programme diet of largely original output which has been geared to a variety of audience categories and has satisfied certain standards of excellence.

In Ireland, the reports of both the Television Commission (in 1959) and the Broadcasting Review Committee (in 1973) emphatically endorsed this form of broadcasting structure as appropriate to Ireland. However, in the last few years, there is increasing evidence on a number of fronts that the old moulds are disintegrating, and rapidly.

The advent of new distribution technologies has considerably upset the status quo. In some cases, direct broadcast satellites will mean an additional five television channels able to serve areas extending well beyond the national frontiers of the countries involved. In other cases, the combination of cable networks and point-to-point communication satellites will sometimes afford more distribution potential than even direct broadcast satellites. Whatever the technical vehicle employed, it will be possible to launch a highly diversified range of new radio and television services, and so progress from a limited supply situation to one of plenty.

It is likely that the new distribution modes will be introduced gradually and that the distribution monopolies and oligopolies will likewise slowly disappear. Despite this relative slowness of the *pace* of change, the *nature* of the changes will be profound for the fundamental reason set out below.

Up to now, the public service broadcasters have enjoyed a near-monopoly of the whole process of broadcasting from studio to home radio or TV set. The only exception has been the advent of independent cable companies and, in recent years, the illegal operators. Now, they must meet the challenge of new national and trans-national services in all parts of the broadcasting chain with technological advances producing a situation of plenty instead of scarcity.

(i) More and more small entrepreneurs will be able to develop video production centres using lightweight equipment which does not require large-scale capital outlay.

(ii) Competition in transmission will be provided by additional cable and satellite organisations using direct broadcast satellites or satellite-to-cable transmission.

16

(iii) There will be competition in the distribution end from Pay TV channels, videodiscs, videocassettes and cinema.

Broadcasters will no longer have exclusive access to the domestic television set; the individual viewer will have a new freedom of choice and as a "consumer" will no longer have television programmes imposed upon him on terms decided by the broadcasters. At the same time the broadcasters will lose the vast captive audiences that were theirs as long as they retained control over the distribution network.

In the past smaller countries such as our own have experienced to an extent the effect of television overspill from larger adjacent neighbours. In the DB satellite age, this will be much more significant and require special attention if we are to retain anything of our own identity in the 21st century.

Far-reaching changes in the conditions under which transmission rights (for imported programmes, sports events, prestige events and the exclusive rights of particular performers) are negotiated can be anticipated.

The law of supply and demand will enable organisers and performers to redress the balance in their favour to a certain extent in negotiations. In some cases competition will lead to a very steep increase in the cost of transmission rights. Similarly, in vying with one another to win over the audience, broadcasters will find themselves having to make heavier and heavier financial commitments for particular programme categories with special audience appeal such as prestige fiction series, cinema co-productions, major documentaries and so on. The old relatively comfortable conventions of the market place, in short, will change drastically.

Income from advertising may be lost, as a result of the competition from alternative channels of distribution. At the same time, TV licence fees may also become a less reliable source, since it is to be feared that, with the proliferation of self-financing services, governments will be more and more reluctant to authorise significant increases in these fees.

What strategy should be adopted to cope with the new and almost frightening situation? I suggest action of two kinds:

— vis-a-vis the public,

— among broadcasters, in the area of programme cooperation.

First and foremost, I believe broadcasters must mount a vigorous campaign to draw the attention of international bodies and national authorities to the following hallmarks of public service broadcasting:

— provision, at a moderate cost, in fact about £1 per week, of a service accessible to all;

— varied and balanced programming designed to meet the needs of all sections of the public and all age-groups;

— impartiality in the presentation of news;

— good balance between informative and artistic programmes;

— dominance of original home productions with all the cultural implications which that carries;

— the entrepreneurial character of public service organisations — employing highly qualified technical staff, more often than not also training them, frequently constituting the country's major employer of performers, and collaborating with national electronic industries in research and development.

It has been possible for these qualities to evolve and be sustained only because a certain balance has been achieved; they could well be forfeited if, with the arrival of new contenders, the market forces were simply to be given free rein. It is essential for a minimum number of rules of play to be prescribed as a means of arriving at a situation of "semi-controlled competition".

In short I suggest that public service broadcasting in Ireland is too valuable a national asset to disappear down the drain as an unfortunate peripheral casualty in an all-out competitive contest between European and North-American giants.

The attention of national authorities must therefore be drawn to the problem of the public service organisations' resources, from two angles:

— The vital importance of creating a sound financial basis for public service organisations at a time when heightened competition will lead to an ever-increasing need for funding in the area of production. To attain this objective the authorities would at suitable intervals have to agree to the necessary increase in licence fees. They would also have to ensure that revenue from advertising is shared equitably through prescribing of minimum rules to ensure balance among national services, meet the problem of transnational advertising, etc.

— Diversification in the activities of public service organisations: experienced operators in the sphere of communications, these organisations ought now to be able to move into new sectors of activity (pay TV, videograms, etc.), which would make their investments in the most expensive productions (dramas, documentaries) more cost-effective.

The European Broadcasting Union could lend its support to such action by the broadcasting organisations; it should take steps to ensure that its various committees are associated with the work of the European institutions which are debating — and may well influence — the structures of the new communications era. The EBU should spotlight the action undertaken to date by its members, and defend their legitimate interests — not by defending the status quo, or by advocating a protectionist policy, but by defending the concept of semi-controlled competition, in the absence of which the 'television of plenty' could well become synonymous with a total decline in programme quality.

Particular attention should be paid to the future of Eurovision which has contributed so much over the last 21 years.

This cooperation could take the form of a European programme of the type prepared during recent experiments, or the pooling of programmes to feed specialised channels. Two aspects of this could merit special attention:

— The setting up of some kind of rights-purchasing body which, through the negotiation of long-term contracts, would enable organisations to secure the transmission rights for major sports or cultural events.

— The promotion of financial cooperation among members in connection with the exchange and/or coproduction of fiction and documentary programmes, thereby enabling organisations either to reduce the cost of such programmes or, while making the same initial outlay, to produce more ambitious programmes which can hold their own with imported foreign productions.

The development of such a policy will inevitably raise problems regarding structures and procedures. It will be necessary to create ad hoc structures with a stronger operational bias, and to give them the freedom to employ more effective management procedures.

In summary we have to re-examine our operating rules and their pertinence for the future. At present these rules are based on national service areas: an organisation acquires transmission rights for its national territory, the cost being directly related to the size of the service area. The advent of satellites and cable systems will lead to much vaster transmission zones, taking in countries affected by unavoidable spillover.

This will mean a whole range of new problems for RTE but also new opportunities. In order to exploit these, we will need to participate in the formation of a responsible and comprehensive national communications policy and to stimulate further enthusiasm from the public at large.

In looking to the future, as for example Kevin Rockett does in his paper, we are obviously charting unknown territory. But we have the model of public service broadcasting before us, and we have in our minds the questions about how that model might, or should, change. This is not only a matter of structures: those have been analysed and challenged before. This collection of papers is additionally valuable, I believe, because it looks at concepts and at 'form and content' — at the culture of public service broadcasting, to use a wider term. Naturally such an approach suggests change, and maybe not all our broadcasters would accept the criticisms or viewpoints expressed. But it is clear that broadcasting has already entered an important new phase which involves and affects everyone in the process, including the people who make the policies and the people who watch the programmes. Seminars such as the IFI Summer School do much to help inculcate such a public attitude and for that reason I am very grateful to the Irish Film Institute for giving me this opportunity of putting forward some thoughts about the future of public service broadcasting and the role we all might play in doing what we can to safeguard it.

2 From Kitchen Sink to Soap: *Drama and the Serial Form on Irish Television*

Luke Gibbons

When Telefís Éireann opened on New Year's Eve 1961, Eamonn Andrews, Chairman of the recently appointed Radio Éireann Authority, noted that in the eyes of many people Ireland was entering a new era: "Cathleen Ní Houlihan . . . was in danger of becoming Cathode Ní Houlihan."[1] The whole way of life embodied in the resonant image of Cathleen Ní Houlihan — the nationalist tradition, the cultural heritage, the primacy of rural values, the repression of sexuality — was about to meet its most serious challenge since the founding of the state. Dire warnings were sounded from all quarters, with the leaders of both Church and State attaching particular gravity to the occasion. Cardinal D'Alton advised Telefís Éireann to adhere to the high ideals of Irish life and warned of the dangers of TV addiction. President de Valera took this a stage further by depicting television as the cultural equivalent of atomic energy in terms of the devastation it could wreak on traditional values: "It can be used for incalculable good," he pointed out, "but it can also do irreparable harm . . . it can lead to decadence and dissolution."[2] Television, he hoped, would devote itself to the expression of the true, the good, and the beautiful, categories not always distinguishable in some of his more romantic evocations of Irish life.

There is little doubt that in the intervening years, television hardly lived up to the elevated role bestowed on it by de Valera. It is possible, in fact, to see in its subsequent operation a parting of ways between the ideals and realities of Irish life which had merged imperceptibly to form some of the most powerful images of Ireland bequeathed by the literary revival. Yet one of the most interesting features of the early years of Irish television is that it was not so much an emphasis on 'the true' — if by that we mean current affairs and documentary — which brought about its departure from traditional cultural norms, but rather developments in such marginal areas as light entertainment (as in the case of *The Late Late Show*), and in some of the less prestigious forms of television drama. From the outset, current affairs was very much at a disadvantage in that politicians were either not available for television discussion — in which case they were replaced by political journalists or specialist commentators — or else their appearance was tightly controlled by party whips, giving programmes such as *The Politicians* the air of a party political broadcast.[3] With current affairs in what was effectively a political quarantine, it is not surprising that other ostensibly less informative and 'serious' television forms stepped into the breach.

There is reason to believe, moreover, that even had current affairs enjoyed a high profile in the opening years of Telefís Éireann, it would still have met with considerable difficulties in broaching some of the more sensitive and controversial areas of Irish society, particularly in relation to family issues and sexual morality. A market research survey undertaken in June 1983 reported that while Irish people were willing to look to television, and to a lesser extent radio and the press, as primary sources of information about politics and current affairs, this deference to the media was less forthcoming in the case of personal or sexual morality.[4] This was not because these areas were considered 'private', but rather because they fell within a different public domain, one which looked to the Catholic Church as a source of guidance and authority. It is to be expected then that when television sought to address itself to these issues, it did not as a rule confront them directly in the form of current affairs or documentary programmes, but rather negotiated them indirectly through areas such as the live chat-show or television serials which were more open-ended and less susceptible to the array of political and legal controls which pervaded Irish television from the outset.[5]

From the Single Play to the Serial: the Development of Drama on Irish Television

Notwithstanding the particular features of the Irish situation, it would be misleading to suggest that the prominent role accorded to television drama in opening up debates on controversial social issues was unique to Ireland. It is almost commonplace by now to point to the extraordinary impact made by single television plays such as *Cathy Come Home* and *Edna The Inebriate Woman* on British public opinion in the 1960s and early 1970s.[6] Many reasons have been adduced to explain how British television drama found itself in this privileged position, acting, in John Caughie's words, "as some kind of cutting edge, working to extend television's social or sexual discourse."[7] In the first place, as Caughie points out, the single television play has traded on the great tradition of high seriousness and creative freedom which has governed thinking about artistic practices in western societies since the Renaissance. This provided a degree of insulation from commercial pressures and managerial intrusion, thus giving television drama a level of prestige and autonomy which is exceptional in terms of marketing outlooks and vertical power structures which characterise broadcasting organisations. Crucial to the flexibility and oppositional stance of the television play, moreover, is the fact that it is script centred, in that the once-off play is seen as the product of a *writer* existing *outside* the institutional structures of the station, as against the director or producer who work within the confines of the organisation.[8]

This tendency to consider the television play as the work of an author or playwright derives, of course, from the stage or mainstream theatre, and this points to a second reason why British television drama made such effective inroads on social and political orthodoxies, particularly in the 1960s. To a greater extent than its American counterpart, which operated in what was largely a cinematic or Hollywood context[9], the British television play was able to draw on developments in theatre, precisely at a time when British drama was undergoing a radical reorientation towards working class life and related social and political issues. The 'theatre of the protest' ushered in by the 1956 production of John Osborne's *Look Back in Anger*, and developed subsequently in the work of playwrights such as Arnold Wesker, John Arden and Harold Pinter, was part of a general rediscovery of working class existence and a questioning of the political consensus which took place in the late 1950s.[10] Underpinned at a cultural level by the critical writings of Raymond Williams and Richard Hoggart, it provided an important thematic focus not only for theatre but also for the novel, cinema and, ultimately, television. Though the connection with high culture is often considered a major restraint on the emergence of popular cultural forms,[11] it is clear that in the particular conjuncture of post-Suez Britain, the ability of television drama to take its terms of reference from radical currents in mainstream theatre worked decidedly to television's advantage, and was at least partially responsible for the success (or notoriety) which it enjoyed during its heyday.

This discussion of British television drama has a direct bearing on the Irish situation, for the emphasis on the more squalid and unpalatable aspects of 'low' life, and the dissenting voices implicit in many of the plays, did not go unnoticed in discussions of Irish television policy during its formative years. Thus in a seminar on Social Communications convened by the Knights of Columbanus in Dublin, June 1964, it is not surprising to find television drama singled out for special attention during the group discussions. As the report of the seminar group on this topic expressed it:

> *There was general agreement that drama had a very definite place in television and that it was desirable to have considerably more drama on television with, however, certain provisos. We felt that we would not like to see a recurrence of what did for a while occur, at least, on the Independent Television programme in England, an excess of*

> *drama devoted to the kitchen sink school, in which the sordid and immoral seemed to be the only things which could be found worthy of the pen of the playwright.*[12]

Commenting on this, the Rev. Luke Faupel, a Catholic communications expert from London, expressed certain reservations even about these qualified recommendations:

> *I am slightly worried at the idea that we should have more drama. I am not at all conversant with the amount of drama that you have, but in England, we have a surfeit of drama. . . . Five plays a week on BBC television and five plays on commercial television, amounts to nearly five hundred plays a year. Are there five hundred playwrights [in Ireland]? Are we not going to descend to the kitchen sink? Are we not going to scrape the bottom of the barrel? It would be a disaster for drama to be overplayed.*[13]

As a counterweight to what he perceives as the excessive realism of British television drama, Fr. Faupel looks to the edifying idealism of the Irish dramatic tradition discerning in it a model for the future course of Irish television drama:

> *I am sure that in this country there must be people – you have a heritage, a dramatic heritage – that can present the concept of the Christian life with all its values, its virtues, its wholesomeness in dramatic form. . . . I am sure you should be very conscious of the dramatic output of a Catholic country like Ireland. I was hoping that you would see a way in which you could support perhaps young script writers . . . especially those people who are content to see virtue in the normal. We have been told that people are disedified with the concentration of (sic) the normalities of our society. . . . Why can't we present the ideal in dramatic form. . . .*[14]

There is a certain irony in the fact that the very strength of the Irish dramatic heritage is invoked in this passage as a means of curtailing the growth of a socially committed dramatic movement, whether it be in theatre or on television. By the 1950s, theatre in Ireland was still languishing in the doldrums of the literary revival, and with the exception of the experimental work of the Pike Theatre and a number of fringe companies, was far removed from the political environment which revitalised British drama.[15] Depictions of Irish life were for the most part confined to an endless treadmill of kitchen comedies and second-rate 'peasant' plays, despite the efforts of playwrights such as M. J. Molloy, Brendan Behan, Gerard Healy and Seamus Byrne to introduce more controversial subjects into the dramatic canon. With the appointment of Hilton Edwards, one of the most distinguished figures in the Irish theatre world, as the first head of television drama in Telefís Éireann, it was evident that the television play was not going to be a vehicle of radical or even muted social comment. Though by no means unadventurous in his projects, staging among other things an ambitious studio-bound version of *Moby Dick*, Edwards' tendency to think of television drama predominantly in studio terms, and his reluctance to use video for editing purposes or for outdoor locations, prevented him from fully utilising the possibilities of the new medium.[16] In a revealing comment some years after leaving RTE, Edwards explained how television's unique ability to bring live coverage of events onto the screen convinced him of the need to clearly demarcate between theatre proper, and socially committed drama which really belonged to the newsroom or the current affairs programme:

> *There is nowadays, caused by the confusion of television, which is also a news medium, a kind of feeling that the drama in the theatre has got to be a kind of newspaper. A lot of people at the Gate are saying to me, why aren't you doing a play about the troubles in Belfast? . . . . I'm afraid that, dramatically, I'm a romantic and an escapist. . . . I think fine plays will be written, but a certain removal in time may be necessary if they are not to be the sort of reportage that I always notice as being the weakness of an O'Casey play.*[17]

Edwards' comments are an important corrective to the view, often found in RTE's Annual Reports in its early years, that financial constraints were the main reason for its poor record in producing television plays.[18] Though the high costs incurred in staging once-off productions were undoubtedly a major contributory factor, an equally important area of resistance would appear to have been the ideological climate (which presided, for example, over the Knights of Columbanus conference quoted above), as well as the undue reliance placed on a moribund, if overpowering, dramatic tradition which felt it had nothing to gain from the new medium. Some measure of the stagnation and complacency which had set into Irish theatre is indicated by the peremptory manner in which one writer, John O'Donovan, dismissed television drama in the course of a survey of nine playwrights conducted by the *RTV Guide* in 1962:

> *Television isn't going to make any radical change in the art of playwriting, and those who pretend that it will are phonies and fakers. Television is a method of presentation, nothing more, nothing less. It presents no challenges in dramatic techniques that have not already been presented by the stage and the cinema. . . . The important thing is **what** you present, not **how** you present it, and no amount of lighting effects, camera gimmickry and hopping from one lens to another will turn a bad play into a good one.*[19]

Of the dramatists questioned, only one, Gerard Healy, seemed fully aware of the wide ranging possibilities afforded by television to break from the deadening influence of mainstream theatre, and to explore new areas of experience in dramatic form.[19] In these circumstances, it is not surprising to find that by the end of 1964, the paucity of original television drama had begun to provoke a response from some of the more critical members of the audience. As one viewer commented in a letter to the *RTV Guide* in November of that year:

> *It is very disappointing to note that in its nearly four years of existence, Telefís Éireann has failed to discover even one Irish playwright of note who writes solely for television. The drama department has been relying regularly on either adaptations of stage plays or imports from the BBC. With rare exceptions it is a proven fact that stage plays are not suitable for TV. . . . Is any effort being made to discover a television playwright, as distinct from a refugee from the stage?*[21]

In her reply to these charges, Chloe Gibson, Head of Drama at Telefís Éireann, pointed out that this outright dismissal of the station's efforts to attract new talent was somewhat unjust, since by then Eugene McCabe, James Douglas and Michael Judge had begun to contribute new original television plays to the station. Nevertheless, the reduction of television to the status of a mere audio-visual aid for existing theatre is evident from the subsequent explanation given for the preponderance of stage adaptations on Telefís Éireann: "These were transmitted," she writes, "in response to widespread demand, particularly from people outside Dublin, who normally have no opportunity of seeing plays produced in the Dublin theatres."[22]

From this remark, it is clear that while some money and energy could be found for television plays, it did not make its way into the commissioning of new material. As the experience of British television showed, such a departure was likely to bring about a rupture with the rural ideals and traditional values which pervaded Irish theatre, opening up new, controversial areas of society to dramatic scrutiny. It was this power of television to focus on contemporary reality, and to probe the darker recesses of social life, which more than anything alarmed the earliest critics of television in Ireland. In 1961, even before Telefís Éireann opened, the Ninth Annual Summer School of the Social Study Conference was devoted to 'The Challenge of Television' in Ireland. At this conference, reservations were expressed about the possible impact of television on two crucial areas of Irish life: the family and the farming community. With respect to the representation of agriculture, the conference noted in a memorandum sent to the Minister for Posts and Telegraphs, and to Radio Éireann, that while television cannot be expected to "hold itself aloof from contemporary problems such as emigration and immigration from rural areas, the relatively depressed state of agriculture and the lack of an image of farming as a 'good life' ", nevertheless, the conference

> *was particularly concerned that the overall impact of the programmes on Irish television should not be such as to convey the image of urban*

or city life as the only desirable one, and that any tendency towards associating an excess of sordid themes with rural life should be avoided.[23]

The conference accordingly expressed the hope that "most" of the programmes on the new television service "including news films would have a rural bias,"[24] an aspiration which was clearly aimed at reinforcing and consolidating the affirmative images of rural life which informed nationalist ideology since the founding of the state. Of particular interest in view of the subsequent development of Irish television drama is the fact that the new station was enjoined to make programmes which would "underline the importance of family unit farm."[25] The centrality of the family in agricultural production meant that the position of women received special attention in this regard, particularly in relation to the need to defend traditional ideals of marriage and motherhood against the incursions of British television drama:

Programmes on married life, which would stress the vocation of motherhood, its satisfactions and trials were they felt particularly necessary, as an antidote to the constant repetition in films and plays from BBC and UTV of the theme of broken marriages and delinquent children. The group also asked that some attempt should be made to provide on the feminine side the equivalent to the various heroes for boys which abound on television screens, such as the Lone Ranger, Maverick, etc. A feminine ideal is a necessity for young girls and the absence of any regular 'heroines' on television screes was stated to be injurious to young girls, particularly teenagers. Serial features on women heroines such as Elizabeth Fry, Edel Quinn, the Angel of Dien Bien Phu, or some of the valiant women of the Old Testament could be attractively presented and should contain enough drama to satisfy even male as well as female viewers.[26]

The most perceptive commentators at the social study conference, however, were not content to direct their criticisms solely at the subject matter or thematic concerns of future programmes, but also turned their attention to the operation of television as a cultural *form,* and particularly to its unrivalled ability to impart knowledge, attitudes and values through the gilded pill of entertainment. In a paper delivered at the conference, and subsequently published as a pamphlet, James J. Campbell pointed out that though the primary aim of television is "to entertain and not to convert" or instruct, nevertheless "television is the most influential factor in education today" in the sense that

the effective vehicle of propaganda [i.e. education] . . . is drama, dramatic representation, which, as every schoolboy and girl knows, poses a problem, sets a conflict and gives us all a thrill (it is hoped) in the working out of the problem.[27]

This corresponds, of course, to the classic definition of narrative, according to which dramatic action takes the form of a movement from order (the beginning), through disorder (the middle) and back to order again (the end) with the resolution of the problem or enigma which impeded the flow of the narrative. This kind of ending or closure brings with it a note of uplift or optimism, and works to best advantage in the single play or self-contained programme. However, the difficulty with television, as Campbell sees it, is that it does not work by instant conversions, but is characterised rather by a "drip effect" which builds up a "composite picture" over a period of time: "The impact," he writes, "is consistent and repeated. It is not a question of a single programme, it is a question of trends and emphases."[28] This makes for a much more diffuse and indeterminate outlook on life, the absence of an affirmative or clear-cut ending tending to leave difficulties and problems unresolved. Hence we have

> *an attitude to grown-up life which is very disturbing, especially among girls for whom there are, as has been said, few positive models on television; we have fear, worry and anxiety about grown-up life and marriage. Young people need reassurance, something positive. What do they get? Uncertainty, fear, anxiety and, of course, no spiritual values, utter materialism.*[29]

Though few examples are cited of programmes with such demoralising tendencies, it is noticeable that the *serial* form is singled out for special mention, "in particular those referring to health and social problems" on UTV or BBC.[30] This concern with the corrosive effects of the serial form is taken up again in another document which emerged from the conference, a fifteen-point memorandum to the Pilkington Committee on Broadcasting which was then sitting in the United Kingdom. In recommending the establishment of a statutory advisory council to monitor broadcasting output, the memorandum goes on:

> *We think that in particular the terms of reference of such a council should include a special mention of the effect of dramatic programmes. . .especially those in serial form . . . we are emphasising . . . that the main impact of television on values and attitudes derives from such programmes.*[31]

It is difficult reading these forecasts of impending doom and dissipation to avoid feeling that they are in some sense self-fulfilling prophecies, the very appropriateness of the fears giving rise to their own realisation. The misgivings about drama, and the identification of the serial as the Trojan Horse of Irish television smuggling in alien attitudes and values; the apprehension about the demise of positive images of the family unit farm, and of traditional female roles, all seem to point towards the inevitable introduction of a farming serial such as *The Riordans*. The wonder is not that the fears and the realities coincided as they did, but that they took so long to do so.

Tolka Row, Family Life and the Urban Serial

One of the most remarkable features of Irish television is that in a country with such a distinguished dramatic tradition, the single play should have been superceded as a critical force in television drama by the much despised serial form. As early as 1968, Tom O'Dea could enquire in his television column in *The Irish Press:*

> *When has RTE's Drama Section broadcast a play that reproduces the attitudes and present temperature of Irish life or a section of it? Now and then **The Riordans** takes up something like the shenanigans that accompany the dismissal of a teacher, or **Tolka Row** tries to dramatise Irish attitudes to the tinkers; but the formal, full-length plays, in which the contemporary, questioning, sometimes dissenting Irishman may be viewed in some depth, are not just there. The most recent Irishman that spoke through RTE's Drama Section was Bernard Shaw . . . . his Ireland is a half-century old.* [31]

It is interesting to note, moreover, that while the critical edge of the serial was readily apparent to those commentators who looked at the new television service from the outside, its full potential in this regard did not impress itself on those working within the station for quite some time. The successes and shortcomings of once-off dramatic productions, for instance, figured prominently in the Annual Reports during the earliest years of Telefís Éireann, but it was not until 1966, when *Tolka Row* was already three years old and *The Riordans* well under way, that the serial received its first honorary mention — being described, somewhat tersely, as the "most popular form of television entertainment". Even Christopher FitzSimon, who perhaps more than any other producer was responsible for the impact made by the serial on Irish television, could still refer to it in 1966 as "the woman's weekly stories of TV," fulfilling their function "which is to provide light dramatic entertainment."[33]

Over the years, and particularly since the growth of American soap operas such as *Dallas* and *Dynasty,* the serial has existed in a kind of critical limbo, its success with audiences being only paralleled by the studied contempt meted out to it in popular television criticism. While much of the animus directed at the serial may be attributed to the elitist values of the 'quality' press, or to the influence of outdated critical precepts derived from high culture, some of the more considered estimates have dismissed the serial as being either a vehicle for a displaced romantic nostalgia (as in the case of a naturalistic serial such as *Coronation Street*), or else as a celebration of American capitalism in its most crass, consumerist forms.[34] Both of these strictures are related, and may be seen as part of a wider general response to the serial, and indeed to all popular or romantic fiction, which finds it wanting on at least two fundamental grounds:

(i) The first is that regardless of its surface attention to detail, and its carefully contrived semblance of reality, the serial manages to obscure and conceal the most important areas of society, in particular the relations of work and production. *Dallas* is ostensibly about oil and economic power, but we seldom see the workforce which allows the Ewings to live a life of endless, if not always carefree, consumption. In this, the occupants of Southfork are no different from other participants in prime-time pastoral as described by Dennis Porter:

> *It should not necessarily surprise if the inhabitants of the land of soap are never observed sleeping, washing, commuting, jogging . . . writing, or even working, and if the closest housewives come to cooking is to pour out a cup of coffee . . . soap opera is . . . a country without history, politics or religion, poverty, unemployment, recession or inflation, and with only minimal references to class and ethnicity.*[35]

While this elision of labour and production, and of political and economic *structures,* is hardly surprising in the heightened melodrama of *Dallas* and *Dynasty,* one would not expect to find it in the documentary style naturalism of *Coronation Street.* Yet as many commentators have pointed out, work for the most part is conspicuous by its absence in this purportedly working class community.[36] Working class existence is defined not in terms of the factory floor, but in relation to the domestic environment of the home, or the personal retreat of the Rover's Return. This brings us to the second major objection which is levelled at the ideological basis of the serial.

(ii) One of the key characteristics of the television serial is the central importance accorded to the family, and by extension, to personal and domestic problems over and against the larger social conflicts which dominate the public arena. This may give rise to a situation in which complex political or economic relations are not so much rendered invisible, as shifted onto a different plane where they are rerouted through an intricate network of emotional or personal entanglements. The private arena, according to Charlotte Brunsdon, "colonises the public, masculine sphere, representing it from the point of view of the personal."[37] Thus in *Dallas* it would appear that whole economic empires can change hands overnight, and the oil industry brought to its knees, so that JR can settle an old score with Cliff Barnes, or assert once more his faltering authority over the wayward and refractory members of the Ewing household.

It is this tendency to explain away the social in terms of the personal which constitutes the basic contradiction of the serial in the eyes of its critics, for in the very process of reducing complex political and economic questions to personal or family dilemmas, we are thereby prevented from understanding their real nature, let alone acting upon them. In modern industrial capitalism, the family is at one remove from the process of production, and is therefore in no position to resolve of its own accord the various social and economic problems which arise in the wider community. It was precisely for this reason that RTE's first important serial *Tolka Row* (1964-1968) came to grief. Based on the day-to-day activities of the Nolan family, who had just moved up in the world from tenement rooms in the Liberties to a new Corporation estate, it tended to present the family not only as the main focus of dramatic interest, but also as the centre of power relations in the community, the place to which everyone turns in the event of personal or social upheavals. "Life in Tolka Row never runs on an even tenor," an article in the *RTV Guide* informs us in 1965, "it is a battlefield 'of crabbed youth and age', of boy breaks with girl, of all hands on deck, lads, the family ship is going on the rocks."[38]

The extent to which the family in *Tolka Row* is bound up with the general concerns of the community is clearly evident in its relationship to the workplace. Jack Nolan works as a foreman in a garage, and in the course of his work is brought into contact with an older workmate, Gabby Doyle. As the story unfolds, Gabby is gradually brought within the ambit of the Nolan household, eventually marrying Stella, Jack's spinster sister, who is living with them in Tolka Row. No sooner has the workplace been reclaimed by the family home in this manner than Sean, the Nolan's modish teenage son, returns from England (to which he had gone after a row with his father) and takes up an apprenticeship in the garage. It is obvious in these circumstances that the workplace is not functioning as an economic unit but rather as a foil for the various liaisons and conflicts entered into by the Nolan family.

This pattern recurs in the work experience of the other members of the family. When Peggy, the Nolans' daughter, is widowed after a brief marriage to Mossy Walker, she takes up a job in the Royal Tara Hotel, and strikes a friendship with Joan Broderick, a young woman on the hotel staff. Joan immediately finds herself drawn into the Nolan circuit, attracting romantic advances not only from Sean but also from his friend Michael Carney. A similar fate befalls Maggie Bonar, a friend of Gabby Doyle's from his homeland in Donegal, who comes on the scene much to the displeasure of the envious and insecure Statia. This rivalry is resolved, or is rather redirected, when Statia and Maggie agree to go into business by forming a domestic employment agency. The very centrality of Statia in the narrative structure, moreover, points to another important aspect of the Nolan household, namely, that it is an extended family catering for relatives and dependents as well as its immediate kin. Not only is Statia a beneficiary in this regard, and to a lesser extent the financially independent daughter and sons, but in the original stage play as conceived by Maura Laverty, Rita Nolan's father, Dan Dempsey, was also part of the household.[38] The family, in other words, not only infiltrates the workplace but also becomes, as Martin McLoone points out (see below pp. 44), a kind of surrogate welfare state, a point of intersection for the various affective and social ties which bind the community. At the heart of this notion of the family, of course, is the mother in the personage of Rita Nolan. As an article in the *RTV Guide* in 1965 expresses it:

> *The focal point of* **Tolka Row** *is Rita Nolan. Rita, who as mother and wife rules the Nolan household, is the peacemaker in times of strife, the source of comfort in times of trouble, and a loyal friend to her relations in Ballyderrig.*[40]

The article goes on to relate that Jack Nolan is about to face a crisis —losing his job as it turns out — which will test his strength and "tax both his common sense and his sense of security. In which case we can rely on Rita to give him support." The fact that in the final episode of the serial Jack Nolan's main activity is washing the dishes after meals, is a testimony to the assertion of the family — and Rita's — values over those of the workplace and the outside community. But it also reveals what was perhaps the underlying structural weakness of *Tolka Row* as a television serial.

In the post mortems which took place after the termination of the serial was announced in March 1968, many explanations were offered for the demise of the programme. Some viewers saw the deterioration setting in after the death of Maura Laverty in 1966, while others, including Carolyn Swift, the script editor, pointed to the inordinately high turnover in the members of the cast.[41] In this respect, the serial was perhaps dealt a mortal blow in 1967 when Iris Lawlor, who played Statia, left the cast to be replaced by another actress. (So irrevocable was the audience's identification of Iris Lawlor with the character of Statia that the waggish TV critic of *The Munster Express* refused to accept the 'new' Statia, contending that *Tolka Row* had gone to the dogs since Gabby Doyle had started sleeping around "with a strange woman passing herself off as Anastatia"!)[42] These setbacks undoubtedly helped to expedite the end of the serial but perhaps the most decisive factor in bringing about its disappearance from the television screens concerned its production context, and in particular the immense strain placed on resources by maintaining two serials (*The Riordans* having started in 1965, one year after *Tolka Row*).

From the outset, *Tolka Row* was greatly hampered by the fact that it was predominantly a studio-bound drama, a limitation which may be attributed not only to the new station's scarce resources, but also to its derivation from a successful stage and television play. Outdoor locations were entirely absent until the second year, but even then they were very infrequent, the action being invariably drawn almost by a gravitational pull back to the Nolan household. (One particular point of frustration for viewers was the inability to peer inside Mrs. Feeney's home next door to the Nolans, and to see the nine "chislers" she was always complaining about!). The restricted use of sets not only made for a certain amount of visual tedium, but also meant that one of the basic dramatic devices of the serial was absent, a communal meeting place such as the Rover's Return in *Coronation Street* or Johnny Mac's in *The Riordans*. As

Christine Geraghty points out, such institutions form the basis of the strong sense of community which exists in the serial, providing a kind of common ground where characters can come into spontaneous or accidental contact, and from which innumerable subplots (and gossip) may emanate.[43] In *Tolka Row,* however, Keogh's pub figures at the very margins of the action, frequented only by the likes of Mrs. 'Queenie' Butler — the official community trouble maker — or Oliver Feeney, Mrs. Feeney's layabout husband.

The lack of a suitable source of common ground or collective meeting-place had far-reaching implications for *Tolka Row,* since it entailed the virtual absence of any wider communal or social setting. As a result, the various social problems thrown up by the action (unemployment, housing and welfare issues, alcoholism etc.) were invariably relocated and displaced onto a family context. "Before the Nolans took their annual leave," wrote Brian Devenney, the *Irish Independent* TV critic, in 1967, "the serial was living off cups of tea and whatever minor excitements could be reported (not shown) within the claustrophic confines of the Nolan family circle and the studio sets available."[44] When the serial returned for the final time in October of that year, it attempted belatedly to adopt a social conscience, addressing itself to controversial issues such as the intolerance shown to itinerants. Far from revitalising the flagging serial, however, this episode and other forays into the darker sides of urban experience — crime, gambling, etc. — only helped to alienate it further from the audience, giving rise to charges that it was unduly preoccupied with the more unsavoury and squalid aspects of working class life. In reply to these objections, Carolyn Swift pointed out that the "passionate belief in the reality of Tolka Row" meant that it had a responsibility "not only to amuse and entertain, but also not to mislead":

> No one feels that Tolka Row should become a documentary about Dublin housing estates. Yet equally it would be wrong to suggest that life in Ballyfermot or Drimnagh or Finglas or Walkinstown presents no problems that cannot be wound up within half-an-hour in a happy ending. No one wishes to introduce the sordid or the vulgar, but we feel we have a duty not to shirk reality, and the truth is that problems in life can be grim at times and are endured with courageous, down-to-earth humour. . . .[45]

The fatalistic implication in this remark that problems are to be endured rather than tackled, and the desocialised character of what is considered an adequate response to urban problems, is hardly surprising, since the attentuated nature of the wider community outside Tolka Row rules out any possibility of concerted social action. As Peter Cleary noted pithily in one of the obituaries which marked the passing of the serial, though it drew attention to a number of social problems "Tolka Row never stepped on anybody's toes."[46]

It is difficult to avoid the conclusion that the family in *Tolka Row* represents not so much the new working class, but an urban residue of a rural family structure.[47] This is apparent not only in the extended nature of the Nolan household but also, as we have seen, in its tendency to derogate wider social functions (having to do, for example, with work or welfare) onto itself, thus giving rise to a misplaced confidence in its own ability to withstand the harsh realities of social and economic change. The existence of a rural backdrop was evident in Maura Laverty's own conception of the serial, and particularly in her characterisation of female roles: while living in Fitzwilliam Street, we are told, she "came to know the horror and warmth of the nearby slums. She found the women there more akin to the countrywomen she had grown up with than anything she found among the city's bourgeoisie."[48] It would seem, moreover, that in the original scenario for the serial, Maura Laverty intended to locate the source of disruption and conflict in the external community, the "menacing" character of Mrs. 'Queenie' Butler ("a holy terror" in the author's eyes) acting as a counterpoint to the more sentimental Mrs. Nolan and Mrs. Feeney.[49] As the narrative developed, however, the character of Mrs. Butler was "softened" and conflict and tension came to reside within the confines of the home, precipitated not only by Statia and the other temperamental members of the Nolan household, but also by the production context which put "the studio bound *Tolka Row* into a sordid bickering second best" to *The Riordans*.[50] According to Wesley Burrowes, who worked as script editor on *Tolka Row* at the height of its popularity, it was this family squabbling and tension which eventually killed the programme.[51] It was time to look elsewhere for a dramatic serial which was more outgoing and less restricted in the range of its concerns. The growing success of *The Riordans* ensured that RTE's Drama Department did not have far to look.

The Riordans: Narrative, Family and Community

The Riordans occupies a central place in the development of Irish television, equalled in importance only by *The Late Late Show* and perhaps the *Seven Days* current affairs' programmes of the late 1960s. It shared with *The Late Late Show* an ability to combine a consistently high level of popularity with an innovative, indeed a pioneering, approach to television production, its outdoor location work in particular attracting interest from television stations all over the world. It is easy to see in retrospect how *The Riordans* was unusually well placed to exploit in full the narrative possibilities of the television serial, but at the time the launching of a popular rural drama involved a number of considerable risks. Not least of these was the likelihood that the serial would be recuperated back into the idyllic versions of Irish life which had dominated traditional representations of the countryside, and which, as we have seen, loomed large in the thinking of the earliest critics of Irish television. *The Riordans* not only managed to steer clear of this romantic ideology, but in divesting rural experience of many of the myths which had surrounded it, made the first major break at a popular level with both the visual and the dramatic legacy of the cultural revival.

One basic point of departure, not only with the romantic image of Ireland but also with some of the standard conventions of soap opera, lay in the unprecedented emphasis which· *The Riordans* placed on work practices, and on the day-to-day routines of farm production. This derived not from any high-minded attempt to bring about a 'realist revolution' in Irish visual culture, such as Courbet and Millet had effected in France in the previous century, but from the rather mundane circumstances which gave rise to the serial in the first place. Initially, *The Riordans* was conceived as a didactic agricultural programme, as a vehicle for imparting, if not smuggling in, the latest information on farm modernisation and machinery. As Gunnar Ruggheimer, the Controller of Programmes responsible for the serial expressed it, the aim of *The Riordans* was

> to get across **surreptitiously** ideas about good farm management and farm practices . . . and to make certain that the actual manipulation of farm equipment is in accordance with normal practice . . . the whole validity of the series, which of course is built on its verisimilitude to a real situation, depends on the actors acting like farmers in every last detail. (My emphasis)[52]

It was this recurrent need for authentic outdoor farm locations which led to the introduction of what was then a completely new concept in television drama, the use of an Outside Broadcast Unit for fictional purposes. This equipment, normally used for televising sporting fixtures and other live events, was unwieldy and cumbersome in the extreme, but by bringing the action out into the open, it dispensed with the convention whereby television drama was incarcerated within a claustrophobic studio setting. By the same token it allowed for different approaches to lighting and editing, but above all, it facilitated a less mannered acting style which helped to break with the Hollywood/Abbey Theatre axis which had up to then monopolised pictorial representation of Ireland.[53] It is not without interest, in this respect, that the basic core of *The Riordans* acting personnel was either new to drama, or else was recruited, not from the Abbey or Gate Theatres, but from the small touring companies which travelled Ireland in the post-war years.

So successful was *The Riordans* in its instructional role that it almost contributed to its own redundancy by paving the way for a regular programme, *Telefís Feirme,* which addressed itself directly to farming matters. By releasing farmers from an unquestioning reliance on time-honoured farming methods, usually underpinned by little more than the authority which the father exercised over the son, *The Riordans* had brought about a situation in which a rural audience was more receptive to social change, and more open to criticising traditional norms. Having set a precedent, therefore, in using the serial as a didactic vehicle, the question arose: where was it to turn next? It would appear that Wesley Burrowes, the writer and editor of the serial, did not need any prompting on this score:

> *It seemed to me that we could now begin to use the agricultural themes as a backdrop to the human and social aspects of rural life. My plan, if it could be called that, was to go on chronicling human relations. But if in the lives of the same people, something of wider social significance were to crop up, then we would prefer to plunge into the heart of the issue rather than skirt round its edges. . . . Already, with . . . episodes . . . about attitudes to the Travelling People, and to a lesser extent in the scenes about coursing, we had gone a little distance in that direction. With that decision, I suppose inevitably, came the beginning of my experience of censorship.*[54]

So a pattern evolved in which the programme began to switch its attention to controversial moral and social issues, but with the same lack of deference to authority and to traditional pieties which characterised its approach to farming matters. It is important to bear in mind, however, that this shift in emphasis did not mean relegating agricultural or economic affairs to a backstage role. Though it maintained the serial's characteristic concern with family life and personal issues, *The Riordans* was also able to relate these directly to wider social and economic questions because uniquely, it afforded the prospect of a world in which personal and familial considerations are intrinsically bound up with the very nature of production.[55] This arose from the fact that it dealt with life on a *family farm,* the basic economic unit of Irish agriculture. The interdependence of home and production on the family farm enabled *The Riordans* to explore complex social and economic problems in the very process of delineating personal and emotional relationships, and without violating the specific character of each domain. It is not surprising in view of its strategic location in the ideological structure of Irish society, that the need for an affirmative image of the family farm was placed so high on the agenda of the earliest critics of Irish television.

The contrast between the favourable social environment of the family farm, and the impersonal nature of industrial work which removes production entirely from the domestic sphere, formed a key element in the defence of rural values which dominated traditional Catholic social teaching, acquiring particular urgency in the changing economic climate of the 1950s. Writing on the rural family in 1952, the Rev. H. Murphy argued strongly against the "individualism" of city life on the grounds that it "destroys the unity of family life and weakens the marriage bond." This situation arises, he contends, when the husband works away from home, but is particularly aggravated by the participation of married women in the workforce, "for then husband and wife are leading to a great extent separate lives: their work, instead of binding them together, separates them." As against this trend, however,

> rural life . . . exercises a much more favourable influence on the family . . . [The] sharing in the occupational activities of the farm binds husband and wife more closely together, for they are linked not only in a domestic but also in a business partnership.[56]

This fusion between 'domestic' and 'business' interests had a considerable bearing on the dramatic economy of *The Riordans,* for it entailed that, in effect, the personal is evacuated of its purely private connotations and is inserted instead into a network of economic and communal relations. In such a public arena, some of the basic set-pieces of the serial form are given a new lease of life: gossip, communal rituals, and the tension between individual freedom and social conformity. In a characteristic scene from one of the earliest surviving episodes of *The Riordans* (10 June 1975), Benjy sets aside his sheep-shearing in the farmyard to tell Fr. Sheehy the news of his engagement to Maggie. On being offered Fr. Sheehy's congratulations, Benjy cautiously refuses to shake hands in case anyone is looking, and the game is given away. Fr. Sheehy has to assure him that only the sheep can see them, before Benjy stops looking nervously around and agrees to stamp this sharing of confidence with the seal of an everyday ritual.

That there are in fact few secrets in Leestown is borne out in the next scene in which we see Benjy, his brother Michael, the local publican Johnny Mac' and a number of others standing around in a group after Mass, discussing the forthcoming party to be held in the Riordans' house. Johnny proclaims grandiloquently that "there is a theory gaining currency that the purpose of the exercise is the announcement of your own impending nuptials" — though mistakenly he thinks it is Michael who is getting married, not Benjy. As if to correct this error, Benjy takes Julia Mac, Johnny's wife, aside in their lounge bar in the next episode, and lets her in on the 'secret' — which in the circumstances is the next best thing to broadcasting it. As Fr. Murphy reminded his readers in his *Christus Rex* article of 1952, in the days before the lounge bar rivalled the church as the main focal point of the community:

> In a rural community . . . all know the difficulties and troubles of each other. . . . The centre of the community is, happily, the parish church and . . . the recurring attendance of the same congregation in the same church fosters fidelity to religious and moral duties. The black sheep is very conspicuous in the country.[57]

The ultimate triumph of community over privacy occurs some episodes later when Benjy and Maggie's idyllic honeymoon in Lahinch is interrupted by the appearance on the scene of Tom and Mary Riordan, Benjy's father and mother, followed by Batty Brennan, the Riordans' aged farm labourer, and his wife Minnie, the local gossip — all converging 'by coincidence' at the holiday resort! It is no wonder Maggie's exasperation shows when she asks Benjy, while they are both lying by the swimming pool: "What are you thinking about?" "Bovine Tuberculosis"comes the reply. Even the memories of the wedding night are not immune from the imperatives of farm production.

This casual exchange is not without significance in the overall context of *The Riordans,* for it draws attention to what is perhaps the most important site of identification between "domestic" and "business" interests in a farming community. This concerns the question of property, and the role of marriage in transferring the family farm to the favoured son who remained at home (often referred to as a "young boy" well beyond his fortieth year).[56] The need to keep the heir apparent or the favoured son on the straight and narrow path, free from the predatory designs of young attached females, fell to the protective influence of the mother, and was a frequent theme in kitchen comedies such as *The New Gossoon* or *The Whiteheaded Boy* which formed part of the repertoire of touring companies before the advent of television.

This fundamental bond between mother and son, in many ways the emotional basis of the family unit farm, received a formidable challenge from *The Riordans.* From the outset, it seemed to set itself the task of replacing this overpowering mother/son relationship by a liaison between the son and an emotional peer of his choice — even if, as in the case of Maggie in *The Riordans,* the girl in question was devoid or economic prospects, having come from an orphanage to work as a barmaid in Johnny Mac's. As Wesley Burrowes describes this conflict of loyalties:

> *If drama depends on tensions, then the relationship between Maggie and her mother-in-law is the stuff of tension.*[59]

The cause of the tension, he goes on to point out, is "the fact that they [both] were rivals for Benjy." Yet if, as Burrowes contends, one of Maggie's great achievements in the programme was "to have been accepted by the public as the rightful and natural contender for Benjy's hand," it is clear that this was far from being an inevita ble outcome. It came at the at the end of no less than eight separate engagements on Benjy's part, not all of them with Maggie but all of them to no avail since, as Burrowes remarks of the various candidates for Benjy's affections:

> *The viewers did not accept them as suitable for Benjy, any more than Mary Riordan did. . . . In the case of Benjy, the mothers of Ireland have to some extent looked on him as a foster-son. And like Mary, they think nobody is good enough for him.*[60]

So desperate was Burrowes to get Benjy married off that at one stage he had Maggie "displaying symptoms which the most sheltered of viewers could hardly mistake". The authorities at RTE felt that this was forcing the issue somewhat, and asked him to drop this interesting line of approach. Burrowes had to consult a doctor to find some alternative explanation for Maggie's symptoms — though the viewers had to wait for three months before the final verdict was delivered.

One might have expected the eventual marriage of Maggie and Benjy to have marked the end of *The Riordans,* and this would undoubtedly have been the case had it been other than a television serial. One of the basic areas of dramatic interest in the serial, however, it that it presents a diffuse, open-ended narrative as distinct from the once-off play or television series which turn for the most part on single, self-contained episodes.[61] Because of the need to establish continuity of action and not just character (as in the series), the serial was prevented from having the kind of *closure* or final *resolution* which brings about the termination of action in a conventional, linear narrative. This absence of an ending, still less of a happy ending, was of considerable importance in a serial such as *The Riordans* which was intent on addressing itself, as we have seen, to social issues. It meant that while there was a continual tendency to open up social problems, and to foreground controversial areas of Irish society, no means were provided of solving them. Not surprisingly, marriage and issues relating to sexual morality in general were at the receiving end of this narrative strategy, the serial bringing to the surface with almost relentless zeal every possible transgression of the traditional Irish family enshrined in the 1937 Constitution.

First to emerge in late 1966 was the issue of illegitimacy, although at this early stage Burrowes was careful to ensure that the unmarried mother was a conspicuous outsider, being introduced into the proceedings as the young English niece of Miss Nesbitt, the upper class Protestant in the serial. Miss Nesbitt's status as an outsider, however, was diminished to some extent by another development taking place at the time. Early in the season, she had accepted (the Catholic) Dr. Howard's proposal of marriage, thus giving rise to a protracted series of negotiations between the various parties, including Fr. Sheehy and Canon Browne (the Protestant vicar), on the implications of a mixed marriage in terms of Catholic teaching. Canon Browne reluctantly conceded to the wedding's taking place in a Catholic church, but expressed his regret that marriage, ostensibly a means of bringing together, should be used to keep them apart by institutionalising some of the more entrenched religious divisions in society. This problem received a final twist some years later when the Howards initiated steps to adopt a child, only to discover that they were prevented as partners in a Mixed Marriage from doing so, under the Adoption Act of 1952. In the circumstances, they had to fall back on fostering a child, a decision which was itself to have unhappy consequences when the natural mother returned some time later looking for her son.

In the meantime, the more unacceptable side of Irish family life had invaded *The Riordans'* household, with the break-up of Jude Riordan's marriage to the agricultural instructor, Jim Hyland. (It is said that this forced Derek Young, the actor who played the part of Jim Hyland, to leave the serial, since in his acting roles outside *The Riordans* he was frequently berated with calls of "Get back to Jude!") Had Jude suffered the ignominy of a marriage separation in isolation, the issue would perhaps have been laid to rest, but there was a widespead angry reaction from viewers when she started keeping company with a divorced Canadian mining executive who was surveying mineral deposits in the Leestown area. On this matter, the viewers were simply re-echoing Mary Riordan's incomprehension at the very prospect that a marriage could break down irretrievably. In an interesting exchange from the episode of June 10th, 1972, which deals with the preparation for Benjy's (as yet unannounced) engagement party, Fr. Sheehy attempts to bring this problem out into the open with an air of feigned innocence, while Mary is serving the ubiquitous cup of tea:

Fr. Sheehy: Have you seen Jude lately?

Mary: Seen Jude? Of course I have Father.

Fr. Sheehy: How are things?

Mary: How are things . . .?

Fr. Sheehy: Just things generally . . .

Mary: Indeed, I don't know what you're talking about Father. There's never anything between Jude and myself that we can't sort out over (looking at her cup and saucer) — over a cup of tea.

In the following episode, Michael attempts once more to probe this raw nerve, forcing Mary to *think through* the problem rather than simply acquiescing to authority and tradition in the search for a clear-cut answer. When Mary expresses her concern that Jude is going from bad to worse by taking up Bridge and "this annulment nonsense," Michael's reply to his mother is that she will have to get used to it:

Mary: I never will.

Michael: Ma, listen. You're against her because it goes against everything you ever believed in, right?

Mary: That's exactly the reason, Michael.

Michael: In other words, its against what the Church taught you—

Mary: Yes it is—

Michael: But all she's doing is asking the Church to decide. She's not against them, its just the opposite — she's going to obey their ruling.

When Mary responds that there is only one ruling the church can make, Michael asks her how would she feel if it came to the worst, and the church annulled the marriage?

Mary: I would feel let down.

Michael:	You wouldn't agree with the decision?
Mary:	No, I certainly would not.
Michael:	But don't you see, then, your argument wouldn't be with Jude, it would be with the Church?
Mary:	Ah! — You're only trying to confuse me with all this smart talk. Its not right, Michael, and it never will be.

Characteristically, the argument is designed to raise questions rather than provide answers, and the problem is left unresolved as the action shifts in the next scene to the more congenial topic of Benjy's forthcoming marriage. As Michael says to Benjy: "When she hears your news, it might take her mind off the Jude business." Mary's respite was to prove temporary, however.

On different occasions, the exploration of other sensitive issues — for instance, the prevalence of sexual ignorance (as in Eamonn Maher's famous question to his wife Eily: "Do you think are we doing it right?") or the problem of "living in sin" and the "kept woman" (as in Paddy Gorey's unwelcome return to Leestown) — helped to dispel the idea that marriages were made in heaven, even if their material purpose was to facilitate the inheritance of various tracts of earth. It was not until difficulties began to surface in Benjy and Maggie's marriage, however, that it became clear that the age of innocence had finally passed in representations of family and rural life in Ireland. The 1974 season revolved around the contentious theme of contraception, precipitated by Maggie's decision to go on the Pill following the complications which attended the birth of her first child. When Maggie turned to Fr. Sheehy for advice on the rights and wrongs of the issue, she was told that there were no pat answers to what was in the last resort a matter of an informed, personal conscience: "I wish I could give you a direct Yes or No Maggie. But I can't. Simply because I'm not you. . . . I can't even mediate for you, in the real sense."[62] By its very non-committal nature, Fr. Sheehy's answer was undercutting a deeply ingrained tendency in Irish Catholicism, evident in the 'question box' or problem pages of popular religious periodicals and Sunday newspapers, to consider complex personal dilemmas as some kind of abstract moral theorems to be solved by having recourse to the appropriate religious 'experts' or authorities.

As the strain began to tell on Benjy's and Maggie's marriage, this non-directive approach was carried over into the treatment of marital infidelity, whether it took the form of Benjy's notorious 'affair in the bushes' with Colette Comerford, or Maggie's more desperate relationship with Pat Barry, who came originally as a farm labourer to replace Benjy on the farm but found himself combining 'business' and 'domestic' interests in a rather unorthodox manner. Throughout the duration of the serial, it was this tendency to open up moral and social issues without closing them off, which drew the most opprobrium, not only from the general audience but also from such forums of liberal opinion as *The Irish Times*. In his TV column in *The Irish Times*, Ken Gray admonished the serial on the grounds that it "constantly throws up contentious and controversial issues and then neatly sidesteps the implications":

> *Many themes with potential for development in the way of social content have been raised, tossed around like a hot potato for a week or two, and quietly dropped.*[63]

In his reply to this criticism, Wesley Burrowes argued that the lack of moral uplift or affirmative endings in the programme arose from its verisimilitude, and its ability to reflect life as it is actually lived in the real world: "I believe that real life provides very few neat wrap-up solutions such as those we are accustomed to in *Kojak* and *The Waltons*."[64] Ironically, however, *The Riordans'* critical edge derived not so much from its transparent rendering of the actual world but from its relationship to *Kojak* and *The Waltons,* that is, from its status *as* a television serial. It was precisely the manner in which it *constructed* its raw material, processing it through generic conventions such as an open-ended narrative, and through a production context which released it from the constraints of Irish theatre and the studio drama, which was responsible for the structured ambivalence which lay at the heart of the serial.

The operation of the dramatic conventions of the serial can be seen to telling effect in the deployment of another formal device which, in a sense, acted as a bridgehead between family and domestic issues and problems having wider social and political import. Much of the documentary feel of a 'realist' continuous serial comes from its use of 'naturalistic time', according to which time in the fictional world of the narrative appears generally to coincide with time in the 'real' world. Thus when it is Christmas time in the outside world, it is also time for seasonal cheer in Coronation Street or Brookside or Leestown. However, this device acquired an extra degree of authenticity in *The Riordans* on account of the need to impart agricultural advice which was both accurate and relevant at the time the audience was viewing the serial. This made for an unusually close correlation between life in Leestown and the everyday concerns of life outside the serial, which in turn open up a valuable space for allowing debates to develop on topical issues almost as soon as they happened. A case in point would be Jude's unhappy experience on moving into a flat in Kilkenny which was subsequently bought by an unscrupulous landlord. This episode represented another setback in Jude's attempt to organise her life after her broken marriage, but was taken out of its domestic setting and invested with direct political significance by virtue of the fact that it coincided with an actual campaign which was being waged in Kilkenny at the time, as part of a concerted national drive against the exploitation of flatdwellers.[65]

42

This was just one of many forays into controversial and at times volatile areas of society made by *The Riordans* in the course of its fifteen years on Irish television. Among the issues which it tackled with varying degrees of conviction were itinerants, wages and conditions of farm labourers (both recurrent concerns because of the presence of Eamonn Maher, Batty Brennan and Pat Barry), mental illness, church control of schools, ecumenism, custodial care of children, gambling, coursing, alcoholism, addiction to tranquilisers — as well as an extensive range of agricultural matters such as farming co-operatives, farm retirement schemes, conflicts over right of way, mining rights etc. At times the sense of immediacy in its treatment of events was such that it was expected to have an almost journalistic topicality, as when on one occasion viewers complained about Tom Riordan's absence from the protests which took place during a national farmer's strike. Indeed, such was its record at intervening in social issues that at times it set the agenda for various public debates. Hardly had Johnny Mac declared war on the rounds system in his pub than this initiative was commended by President Childers, who began his own campaign to beat the rounds system. At a more serious level, the Minister for Lands, Tom Fitzpatrick, had occasion to cite Benjy's protracted struggle to gain a majority shareholding on the family farm, as an argument for early farm retirement to facilitate progressive young farmers.[66]

It is perhaps in the general area of family politics, rather than in its treatment of any one particular issue, that *The Riordans* made its most valuable contribution to Irish society. By disengaging the rural family from the cycle of inhibition, authority and conservatism in which it had been traditionally enclosed, it made deep inroads on a dominant ideology which looked to the family — and indeed the family farm — as the basic unit of Irish society.[67] Unlike the conventional soap opera (or for that matter *Tolka Row*) which runs the risk of mystifying and desocialising power structures by reducing social and economic relations to the vicissitudes of individuals, *The Riordans*' concern with the rural family brought it out of the individual private arena and into a wider social domain.

See over p. 44, Production Context and Narrative Structure of The Riordans.

Yet it is important to point out that despite the centrifugal movement away from the family,[68] one of the striking features of *The Riordans* is the relative absence of forms of collective action which transcend familial or affective ties. Though Jude's dispute with the rackrenting landlord coincided with the activities of an organised flatdwellers' campaign in the 'outside' world, it was not approached from this angle within the story but rather mediated through Tom Riordan's intervention, both in his role as father and as an independent County Councillor. In the episode of 10 June 1973 adverted to above, a related housing issue (in this case the shortage of homes for old people) is taken out of the area of impersonal

Production Context and Narrative Structure of *The Riordans*

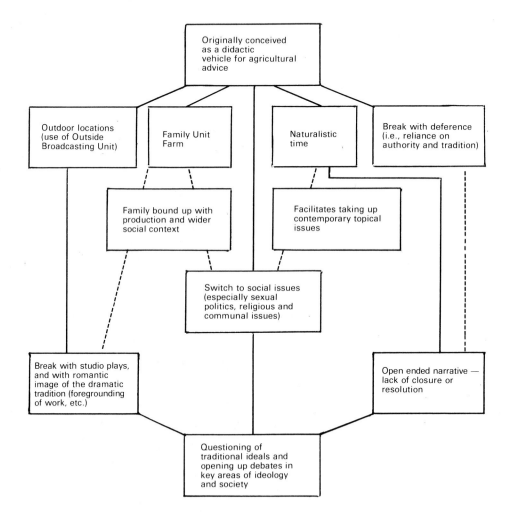

Originally conceived as a didactic vehicle for agricultural advice

Outdoor locations (use of Outside Broadcasting Unit)

Family Unit Farm

Naturalistic time

Break with deference (i.e., reliance on authority and tradition)

Family bound up with production and wider social context

Facilitates taking up contemporary topical issues

Switch to social issues (especially sexual politics, religious and communal issues)

Break with studio plays, and with romantic image of the dramatic tradition (foregrounding of work, etc.)

Open ended narrative — lack of closure or resolution

Questioning of traditional ideals and opening up debates in key areas of ideology and society confrontation when Fr. Sheehy seeks to persuade Michael Riordan to establish a voluntary housing co-operative venture along the lines of the Christian Community Action group which was operating successfully elsewhere in the country.

It is difficult to escape the conclusion that while solidarity or collective effort is easily mobilised around consensual or communal issues, it is less forthcoming at an adversary level, or in the case of social divisions or conflict. It is instructive, for example, that while the community rallies around Batty Brennan, the Riordan's aged farm labourer, in his hour of need when he hears the news of his wife's relapse in hospital, this occurs in Johnny Mac's pub, at the level of consumption, one might say, rather than production. When problems arise relating to his — or more particularly Eamonn Maher's — status as a farm labourer, this collective support is less visible. Though Eamonn has recourse to the rulings of the Agricultural Wages Board in his numerous rows with Tom Riordan over wages and conditions, his response usually takes the form not of Union activity but of the ineffectual "expressions of annoyance, boredom and chafing against restraint" which vitiate social conflict in Arensberg and Kimball's description of the Irish rural community.[69] In the long term, Eamonn overcomes the problem by securing his own farm, thus exemplifying the pattern noted by David Fitzpatrick whereby "social mobility is hostile to class-collective action [in the rural community], since it encourages queue-jumping rather than conspiracy among frustrated queuers to take over the bus".[70] As Miley Byrne says to the disgruntled Pat Barry in *Bracken,* who, having just made the transition from farm labourer to smallholder, complains about the fact that seventy per cent of the land of Ireland is owned by five per cent of the people: "Do you know all this thing about the five per cent — the rich men, the Dalys. You don't want all that money and wealth shared out. You just want them to move over, to make room for yourself." Indeed, such is Eamonn Maher's ability to make room for himself that from his initial position as an itinerant, he ends up in a protracted relationship with Colette Comerford, the daughter of the wealthiest farmer in the district.

Personal relationships also provide Batty Brennan with a means of escape from the confines of his class position — in this case his marriage to Minnie, owner of Leestown's Home Bakery "with Select Accommodation above." Yet while class tensions are blurred and defused in this manner, the whole narrative thrust of *The Riordans* at another level is to close off this esape route by undermining at every turn the central role of marriage as a force of reconciliation in the community. It is revealing that in the case of Jude and Paddy Gorey, for whom marriage is ruled out as an option, their inability to negotiate this terrain is accompanied by a descent in social status and esteem. For similar reasons, characters like Michael Riordan and Willie Mahoney, for whom marriage is an external possibility rather than a practical reality, move around in a kind of social cul-de-sac, always promising but never delivering. In all of these situations, problems are thrown up which, with the disintegration of familial structures, call for forms of resistance or concerted action which confront advertisity or conflict at a more engaged, organised level. The need for campaigns around issues such as divorce, contraception, and unemployment is frequently alluded to, but is never fully developed. Collective responses of this kind resemble those characters who, though temporarily removed from the serial, always maintain, in Jean O'Halloran's words, "a peripheral presence,"[71] hovering at the edges of the action even when they do not directly manifest themselves.

Bracken: **Melodrama and the Disintegration of Family and Community**

By the time *The Riordans* was taken off the television screens in 1979, the image of the Irish rural family had travelled a long way from the sentimental conceptions of family and community which informed the earliest critical appraisals of Irish television. Almost every variation on the theme of the happy Irish home had been given an airing, to the extent that when *The Riordans* was replaced in 1980 by a new serial *Bracken,* all but the faintest traces of the family unit farm were excised from view. In *Bracken,* the brooding figure of Pat Barry returns from his job as a labourer on Tom Riordan's farm to take over the diminutive holding left to him and his emigrant brother on his father's death. Though we are led to believe that only the mountain of Slieve Bracken separates Leestown from the townland of Bracken, to pass from one community into another is, in effect, to enter a new moral continent. In *Bracken,* there is a narrative shift from a naturalistic to a melodramatic genre, albeit in a less-heightened, restrained form. The family, where it is present at all, is a site of internecine struggle and personal intrigue, and its internal divisions are no longer inscribed on the wider social and ideological conflicts taking place in the community. By the same token, the idea of community is itself attenuated, and recedes into the background as a menacing presence, an aggregation of glancing looks and mumbled conversation which only impinges on the action in the form of collective violence.

Bracken in a sense takes up where *The Riordans* and *Tolka Row* leave off. The conflict between Pat Barry and Daly, the rancher farmer manipulating the community for his own ends, is not mediated by family ties or domestic considerations, except insofar as Louise, Daly's daughter, is a pawn in his calculations. For this reason, it is not surprising that in *Bracken* there is a complete eclipse of the mother figure, the most powerful source of cohesion in the community. The only approximation to the mother role is the insipid Jill Daly, Louise's mother; but she is merely a cipher for her husband's opinions, is inefficient as a wife and as a protector of her daughter's interests, and in the end throws off the last vestiges of motherhood when Daly abandons her and she has an affair with Pat Barry.

46

Just as Jill is an affront to the role of mother as represented by Mary Riordan (or Rita Nolan), likewise her daughter Louise is far removed from the homely and unaffected Maggie in *The Riordans*. Louise's presence invariably emits an erotic charge which seems totally at odds with the maternal instincts which come so naturally to Maggie. To a certain extent, this sexual profile is imposed on Louise in that as a daughter rather than a son, she is not directly entrusted with responsibility for producing the heir to the Daly estate. As such, her sexuality, like that of Peggy in *Tolka Row*, is less defined by the procreative role which circumscribed Maggie's behaviour in *The Riordans* — or at least did until Pat Barry came on the scene.

Pat Barry, with little to worry him by way of property except an impoverished sheep farm, is not unduly burdened either by the task of securing his line of succession — nor is it likely that others will be attracted to him because of his wealth and material possessions. Marriage for him is merely a form of social mobility, a means of advancing his own interests by what he sees as the only route open to the man of no property. His sexual appeal, understated at first, proves to be his passport to the big house, bringing about an affair not only with Louise, but also with her mother and, for good measure, Louise's best friend Eve who momentarily diverts Pat from his more profitable emotional engagements.

Insofar as marriage and the family manifest themselves at all in *Bracken*, it is in the form of patriarchal relations. However, father figures, far from being centres of authority and action, are repeatedly brought down in the world and reduced to a state of abjection and powerlessness. It was Pat Barry's neglect of his own father through his departure for Leestown which led to his father's loss of interest in life and to his eventual death. A similar fate befalls the unctuous Dinny Byrne whose son Miley leaves him to go to England on finding out about his underhand dealings with Ned Daly. Daly's own fortunes take a dramatic downturn as he becomes increasingly isolated from his wife and daughter, and returns to his old haunts in England in an attempt to recover the self-respect he once enjoyed. In a dingy pub on a backstreet, his path crosses that of the hapless Dinny, aimlessly searching for his missing son. Bracken, clearly, is no country for old men.

*   *   *   *   *

It is interesting to revisit Bracken, Leestown and Tolka Row in the light of the renewed assaults which have been levelled at imported melodramatic serials such as *Dallas* and *Dynasty* for corrupting the moral fibre of the Irish nation. These charges seem to have gained impetus from the recent constitutional referendum on abortion, and have been a regular feature of popular analyses of the drift away from traditional Irish attitudes towards sexuality. As Frances O'Rourke puts it in the course of a discussion on the causes of teenage pregnancies in Ireland:

> *If kids are sex mad, look at TV ads, look at **Dallas**, look at our place in Western pop culture and at human nature for some reasons why.*[72]

As in the case for the argument that the demand for abortion in Ireland was being imposed from abroad on an unsuspecting Irish public, likewise "bed-hopping soaps" (to quote Frances O'Rourke's graphic phrase) are singled out as the scouring agents which have tarnished irretrievably images of family and community in Ireland. It is difficult to escape the conclusion that commentators here are searching in vain abroad for what they can readily find at home. In an astute observation in a recent issue of the Dublin *Northside Express,* the television critic relates how he listened to a letter from "an outraged licence-holder" on the RTE programme *Mailbag* who *"complained that RTE should screen more home-produced goodies like **Glenroe** and **The Riordans**. Programmes like **Dallas**,"* he complained *"are destroying the moral fibre of this country."* While I sympathise with him about **Dallas**, *"we would like to point out that between **Glenroe**, **The Riordans** and **Bracken**, every form of vice reasonably imaginable has been screened. We've had extra-marital sex, adultery, drunkeness, pub brawls; hardly the sort of stuff to improve the moral fibre."*[73]

REFERENCES

1. For the text of Eamonn Andrews' speech, see "One of the Most Exciting Years of my Life", *RTV Guide,* 12 January 1962, p. 3.

2. *Irish Times,* 1 January 1962, p. 3. For full text of de Valera's speech, see Appendix 1.

3. David Thornley, "Television and Politics", Administration, Vol. 15, No. 3 (1967), p. 218. At the time of writing, the author had just joined the *Seven Days* programme whose turbulent history placed current affairs firmly on the map of Irish television.

4. "MRBI 21st Anniversary Poll", *Irish Times,* 27 June 1983, p. 6.

5. For some interesting observations on this point, see T.J.M.S., "Success of the Indirect Approach", *Irish Catholic,* 18 April 1968, p. 1.: "One of the paradoxes of television is the fact that the most successful way to present quite serious ideas is often through the lightest of entertainment. . . . To put across very serious ideas on television, the obvious way would seem to be to present experts on the subject either in interviews, or involved in a debate or discussion. . . . But when the same serious views are neatly woven into a popular entertainment programme, like *Tolka Row,* the impact on the public covers a much wider range of viewers, and in many cases makes a much more definite impact."

6. See George Brandt (ed.), *British Television Drama* (Cambridge: Cambridge University Press, 1981), especially Martin Banham's article on Jeremy Sandford pp. 194-217.

7. John Caughie, "Progressive Television and Documentary Drama", *Screen,* Vol. 21, No. 3 (1980), pp. 36-9.

8. W. Stephen Gilbert, "The TV Play: Outside the Consensus", *Screen Education,* No. 35 (Summer, 1980), pp. 36-9.

9. Caughie, op. cit., p. 16. Among the directors who made the transition from television to cinema were Arthur Penn, Robert Mulligan, John Frankenheimer, Sidney Lumet, and George Roy Hill. See Michael Kerbel, "The Golden Age of TV Drama" in Horace Newcomb (ed.), *Television: The Critical View* (New York: Oxford University Press, 1982).

10. See the remark by Sydney Newman, the Canadian producer who was perhaps the most significant figure in the development of British television drama in the late 1950s and 1960s: "I came to Britain at a crucial time in 1958 when the seeds of *Look Back in Anger* were beginning to flower. . . . I am proud that I played some part in the recognition. The working man was a fit subject for drama, and not just a foil in a play on middle-class manners." Quoted in Edwin Eigner, "British Television Drama and Society in the 1970's," in James Redmond (ed.), *Themes in Drama* (Cambridge: Cambridge University Press, 1979), p. 212. See also Caughie, op. cit., pp. 18-9.

11. For the most influential exposition of this argument, see Walter Benjamin, "The Work of Art in the Age of Mechanical Reproduction" in *Illuminations*, trans. Harry Zohn (London: Fontana 1973).

12. "Dublin Discussion on the Media", *Christus Rex*, Vol. XIX, No. 1 (1965), pp. 17-8.

13. Ibid., pp. 24-5.

14. Ibid, p. 24.

15. Christopher Murray, "Irish Drama in Transition 1966-1978", *Études Irlandaises*, No. 4, Nouvelle Serie (December 1979), pp. 289-90. See also Terence Brown, *Ireland: A Social and Cultural History 1922-79* (London: Fontana, 1981) pp. 319-20.

16. Hilton Edwards, "The Problems and Possibilities of TV Drama", *RTV Guide*, 26 January 1962, p. 4.

17. Hilton Edwards, "Drama on Television", *Aquarius* (1973), p. 108.

18. See Annual Reports for 1962 and 1963. In 1965 the shortage of original script writers for television is also cited.

19. "How will Irish drama be affected by the coming of Telefís Éireann?", *RTV Guide*, 26 January 1962, p. 3.

20. See Healy's comment: "I'm absolutely all for television. Any extra market for dramatists is definitely a good thing. Television is a much more flexible medium than the theatre, and the plays we will see from abroad will help our young writers to get away from the kitchen sink (i.e. kitchen comedies?) to explore new settings. I believe that television will encourage our writers to show us aspects of Irish life that are neglected by the theatre." Ibid.

21. Letter from Richard Elvine, *RTV Guide*, 27 November 1964, p. 2.

22. Letter from Chloe Gibson, *RTV Guide*, 4 December 1964, p. 2.

23. "Memorandum on Television to (i) the Minister for Posts and Telegraphs (ii) Radio Éireann, from the Social Study Conference Ninth Annual Summer School, August 1961", reprinted in James J. Campbell, *Television in Ireland* (Dublin: M. H. Gill & Son Ltd., 1961), pp. 27-8.

24. See the detailed report of the Conference in Ita Meehan, "The Opinions of the Citizen", *Christus Rex*, Vol. XVI, No. 2 (1962), p. 103.

25. Ibid.

26. Ibid., p. 105.

27. Campbell, op. cit., p. 8.

28. Ibid., p. 10.

29. Ibid.

30. "Memorandum to the Minister for Posts and Telegraphs", *Ibid.*, p. 26. It is interesting to find precisely these aspects of *Tolka Row* singled out for mention, albeit in a more affirmative sense, by the television critic for *The Irish Catholic* some years later: "I suspect, for example, that the recent editions of *Tolka Row* watched primarily as entertainment, brought to many people who have little time for "serious" programmes, some serious ideas about the general public attitude to psychiatry and mental health; about the plight of some of our people struck by poverty; and about the average citizen's concern or lack of concern with the basic precept of charity." (T.J.M.S., "Success of the Indirect Approach", op. cit.).

31. "Memorandum to the Pilkington Committee on Broadcasting from the Social Study Conference (Ireland), August 1961", Ibid., p. 22.

32. Tom O'Dea, "A Taste of Summer", *The Irish Press,* 20 April 1968, p. 11.

33. "Profile: Christopher FitzSimon", *RTV Guide,*18 February 1966, p. 7.

34. For comments of the nostalgic milieu of *Coronation Street,* see Raymond Williams, *Television: Technology and Cultural Form* (London: Fontana, 1974), p. 61, and Richard Dyer, "Introduction" to Dyer et al., *Coronation Street* (London: British Film Institute, 1981), pp. 4-5. For a critique of the 'consumerist' basis of American Soap-opera, see Peter Conrad, *Television: The Medium and its Manners* (London: Routledge and Kegan Paul, 1982), pp. 66-87, and "A Screenful of Dollars", *The Observer,* 16 May 1982, p. 28.

35. Dennis Porter, "Soap Time: Thoughts on a Commodity Art Form", in H. Newcombe (ed.) op. cit., p. 125.

36. R. Dyer "Introduction", in Dyer, op. cit., pp. 4-5 and Marion Jordan, "Realism and Convention", Ibid., pp. 31-3.

37. Charlotte Brunsdon, "*Crossroads* — Notes on Soap Opera," *Screen,* Vol. 22, No. 4 (1981), p. 34.

38. "Tolka Row", op. cit., p. 12.

39. Christopher FitzSimon, "Tolka Row", *RTE Guide,* 17 May 1968, pp. 6-7.

40. Norman Smythe, "Tolka Row", *RTE Guide,* 23 September 1966, p. 7.

41. Carolyn Swift, "Old Friends and New Faces", *RTE Guide,* 6 December 1967, p. 16.

42. "Video News", *Munster Express,* 27 October 1967, p. 11.

43. Christine Geraghty, "*Brookside* — No Common Ground", *Screen,* Vol. 24, No. 4-5 (July-October, 1983), p. 137.

44. Brian Devenney, "Television Commentary", *Irish Independent,* 21 October 1967, p. 11.

45. Carolyn Swift, "150 Episodes of Tolka Row", *RTE Guide,* 10 November 1967, p. 11.

46. Peter Cleary, "Passing of Tolka Row", *Sunday Independent,* 3 March 1968, p. 25.

47. This is not to say that *Tolka Row,* or for that matter other representations of urban life which display residual rural structures, necessarily distort the nature of working class experience in Dublin. It may be, indeed, that *Tolka Row* was attempting to articulate what A. J. Humphreys refers to as the "radical continuity between the general pattern of the family in Dublin and the rural community" (Alexander J. Humphreys, *New Dubliners: Urbanisation and the Irish Family* (London: Routledge and Kegan Paul, 1966). p. 234. See also pp. 250-1). Humphreys instances religious belief, kinship, solidarity, filial piety and neighbourliness as cases in point, but draws attention nevertheless to the far-reaching effects on family organisation, paternal authority, marriage patterns, and welfare dependency brought about by the loss of the family's function as a unit of economic production.

48. "Profile: Maura Laverty", *RTV Guide,* 13 May 1966, p. 15. It is interesting to note that Rita Nolan is represented as having rural origins — in County Kildare — while Gabby Doyle and Maggie Bonar are from Donegal, to which they return at the end.

49. See the interesting letter by Paddy Corrigan to the *RTE Guide,* 31 May 1968, p. 2.

50. Brian Devenney, "A Critic's Top Ten", *RTV Guide,* 29 April 1966, p. 4.

51. Wesley Burrowes, *The Riordans* (Dublin: Gilbert Dalton, 1977), p. 6. The analysis of *The Riordans* which the following section is greatly indebted to Mr. Burrowes' lively account of his association with the serial.

52. Ibid., pp. 2- 3.

53. "The Riordans: Telefís Éireann's new serial begins at 7.15 on Monday", *RTV Guide,* 1 January 1965, pp. 12-3.

54. Burrowes, op. cit., p. 18.

55. It would seem that a large measure of the success of a serial such as *Angels,* which was set in a hospital, was due to the fact that it was located in the workplace. However, even in this situation there is a clear demarcation between the public occupations and the private lives of the characters — something which does not hold in the family unit farm. *Crossroads,* set in a motel, would perhaps be the nearest to a combination of workplace and personal lives in a British serial.

56. Rev. H. Murphy, D.D., "The Rural Family: The Principles", *Christus Rex,* Vol. VI, No. 1, p. 7.

57. Ibid., p. 10.

58. Conrad M. Arensberg, *The Irish Countryman* (New York: American Museum Science Books Edition, 1968), pp. 66-7.

59. Burrowes, op. cit., p. 92.

60. Ibid.

61. For an excellent account of the narrative structure of the serial, see Christine Geraghty, "The Continuous Serial — A Definition", in R. Dyer, *op. cit.,* pp. 9-27.

62. Burrowes, op. cit., p. 86.

63. Ibid., p. 91.

64. Ibid. See also his comment elsewhere: "I have been criticised for not tying up loose ends in plots or not striving for a satisfactory solution. This is precisely because they are not plots. They are characters in real-life situations and as you well know, life doesn't tie up its loose ends." ("Riordans characters act real-life situations", *Irish Farmer's Journal,* 25 November 1967, p. 24).

65. Burrowes, op. cit., pp. 91-2.

66. Ibid., p. 101.

67. See the classic sociological analysis of the central importance of the family in the Irish social structure, Conrad M. Arensberg and S. T. Kimball, *Family and Community in Ireland* (Cambridge: Harvard University Press, 1940).

68. See Jean O'Halloran, "Theme and Process in Television Drama: The Case of Irish TV", (Unpublished dissertation, NIHE, Dublin), p. 51.

69. Arensberg and Kimball, op. cit., p. 174.

70. David Fitzpatrick, "Class, Family and Rural Unrest in Nineteenth-Century Ireland", in P. J. Drudy (ed.), *Ireland: Land, Politics and People* (Cambridge: Cambridge University Press, 1982), p. 55.

71. O'Halloran, op. cit., p. 32.

72. Frances O'Rourke, "Facing up to the Half-Way Halt", *Sunday Press,* March 11, 1984, p. 15. Similar sentiments are contained in an article one week earlier, Maryanne Heron, "Whatever have we done to sex in Ireland", *Irish Independent,* 3 March 1984, p. 7.

73. *Northside Express,* 1 December 1983, p. 4.

3   Strumpet City -
The Urban Working Class on Irish Television

Martin McLoone

Introduction

In the Spring of 1980, RTE screened its own seven part adaptation of James Plunkett's novel *Strumpet City*. Originally published in 1969, the novel deals with the years of labour agitation in Dublin between 1907 and 1914, culminating in the lock-out of September 1913 when large sections of the Dublin working class were reduced to starvation and the labour movement to political defeat. At the time of its publication, the novel was a world-wide best-seller as well as a universal critical success. Indeed, the original paperback edition of 1971 declared on its front-cover — "The greatest epic novel since Dr. Zhivago".[1] It was precisely this language of scale and superlative that was attached to the television adaptation.

The serial was heralded as a major breakthrough in Irish television drama.[2] It was presented as such by RTE and was received as such by critics, commentators and the general audience. There was, for example, a lot of emphasis on production details.

It was the most expensive Irish television drama production to date, costing £1 million according to RTE's own figures. It was shot entirely on film and the Hollywood-style proportions of the production were emphasised by the casting of Peter O'Toole as the labour leader, Jim Larkin and by the presence in a cameo role of Peter Ustinov.

There can be no doubting the institutional importance of *Strumpet City* for RTE. The serial was planned as part of an overall strategy by the station to break into the international market. In a sense it was a gamble to carry on its own the huge costs of this production, in order to establish its credentials world-wide as a source of quality television drama. The escalating costs of drama production and the squeeze on income brought about by the general recession made the prospect of international co-productions financially very attractive.

By 1980, anyway, over 40% of RTE's audience was receiving good quality reception from BBC and ITV, mostly through cablesystems, and if it were to compete on reasonable terms with British television it was felt that drama production would have to be on a scale equivalent to that of the competition. Finally the returns to the British channels of overseas sales, especially to English-speaking countries, was another incentive to plan drama production with the international market in mind.

In the event the gamble would seem to have paid off. *Strumpet City* was sold extensively throughout the world, covering its initial production costs by 1982. It was sold, for example, to Independent Television in Britain for a reputed £75,000 per episode. (It was a major disappointment to all involved in the production that, by and large, the ITV companies chose to show *Strumpet City* at off-peak times —London Weekend Television, for example, screened it after 11 p.m. on Friday evenings and Ulster Television in a mid-week, mid-afternoon slot.) However, some compensation was Channel Four's repeat screening in the early Summer of 1984.

More importantly though for RTE drama, the success of *Strumpet City* opened the way for the international co-productions that had been hoped for. In 1982, for example, RTE set up a three-way co-production deal, involving French channel FR3 and Channel Four in Britain, to produce a six-part adaptation of Thomas Flanagan's historical novel *The Year of the French.*[3] *The Irish R.M.* was co-produced with Channel Four, and proved to be one of the new Channel's most popular programmes during its first year of operation. In 1983, co-productions included the critically acclaimed four-part series *Caught in a Free State,* again with Channel Four and a BAFTA-award winning short film *The Ballroom of Romance* with the BBC.

The success of this strategy for RTE has had unfortunate consequences. Already, it has meant a severe cut-back in domestic drama production and a virtual end to co-productions with independent Irish film-makers, a particularly unfortunate consequence at a time of greater optimism and increased activity in the independent sector. More problematically, there is now an urgent need to analyse and assess these international co-productions in terms of the images of Ireland that are being produced and to gauge the wider cultural implications of television drama that is aimed increasingly for international audiences.

However, in terms of the strategy which it initiated, there is no doubt that *Strumpet City* has been a conspicuous success for RTE and the international prestige of Irish television drama today has never stood higher.

The emphasis on *Strumpet City* has, therefore, almost always been on its institutional importance to RTE, and the underlying economic reasons for adopting the drama policy which this implies. However, I want to approach an analysis of the production from another direction altogether, and in doing so I want to situate *Strumpet City* in a wider cultural and historical context.

The real significance of the serial lies in the way in which it inserts itself into Irish culture in a specific way and at a specific historical moment. For I want to make the case that despite the rather hard-nosed practicality of its conception, *Strumpet City* stands as a paradigm of the ruptures and contradictions of contemporary Irish society and that if it marks a turning point for Irish TV drama, it stands also as a consummation of what I would call the "ideological project" of Irish television over the last two decades.

1. Wider Cultural Context — Constructing the Consensus

> ... *impoverished as the people are* ... *the outward aspect is a pageant. One may see processions of young women riding down on Island ponies to collect sand from the sea-shore or gathering turf, dressed in their shawls and in their brilliantly coloured skirts made of material spun, woven and dyed by themselves* ... *Their simple cottages are also little changed. They remain simple and picturesque. It is only in such places that one gets a glimpse of what Ireland may become again.*[4]

These sentiments of Michael Collins neatly encapsulate a number of the dominant characteristics of Irish nationalism which developed in the late 19th century, informed the armed struggle in the early twentieth century and remained central mythologies to the Irish state for over forty years after independence was achieved in 1922. This was Collins' version of the new Ireland — Eamon de Valera, who presided over the new state in one capacity or another for forty years, referred to "frugal self-sufficiency" as the central characteristic of his programme.[5] Despite their political disagreements over the terms of the 1922 Treaty, both men shared common cultural conceptions.

Implicit in Collins' vision is the same concept of frugal self-sufficiency — a way of life that is hard, yet noble, a way of life that has beauty and primitive virtue; a life of unchanging stability, sunk deep in tradition. Two crucial ideological concepts are summarised here.

First, there is the resonance of the word "again". Irish nationalism is built on the fundamental notion of an historic Irish nation that had existed once and will do so again. It was the task of cultural nationalist movements in the 19th and early 20th century to give this concept some cultural and historical legitimacy and Collins here gives expression to the way in which this was achieved.

Ireland was presented as some kind of rural utopia, or Garden of Eden which, if a little harsh, could be nonetheless, free, self-sufficient, Irish and virtuous. Why virtuous?

I think the second ideological concept here is the displacement of women into symbols of Ireland itself — in Collins' version, young Irish girls, asexual in their beauty and chaste in their deportment. Cultural nationalism has made great play with the metaphor of Ireland raped and debased by English influence. In offering myths of Mother Ireland, or Cathleen Ní Houlihan, this dual concept of chastity and rural utopia is posited against all that England stood for. These ideologies ultimately reflect the social forces which amalgamated to carry through the successful nationalist revolution of 1922 — the social conservatism of the urban bourgeoisie, the entrenched traditionalism of the rural bourgeoisie and small farmer and the pervasive power of a puritanical Catholic Church.

It was no surprise then that the State which emerged in 1922 and was consolidated by de Valera from 1933 onwards should show the same kind of social conservatism and Catholic authoritarianism. As Joseph Lee explains:

> 'Traditional' Irish society achieved singular success in excluding ethics from the sphere of religion, largely confining the concept of morality to sexual morality and banishing from the agenda of moral discourse doctrines potentially subversive of the material interests of the dominant social elements. 'Traditionalists' naturally strove to divert hierarchical concern away from the dangerous area of public morality, and revert to the safe ground of sexual morality.[6]

The potentially subversive doctrines which Lee refers to are significant in placing *Strumpet City* in its wider cultural context. The most threatening doctrines are, of course, those associated with the labour struggles of the urban working class. It was the achievement of the nationalist alliance of class interests that it was able to detach urban working class issues from the national struggle and establish a consensus around the concept of the historic Irish nation. And it was the specific task of cultural nationalism to provide the images and myths of rural Ireland that elided the urban working class from Irish culture.

In this sense, then, even the title *Strumpet City* is charged with ironic ideological import. The city was not only the site of these potentially divisive doctrines, it was also the site of loose sexual morality. Another connotation of the strumpet epithet is that if the Irish countryside maintained the purity of the historic Irish nation, the city, a product of English influence, had prostituted itself to the foreigner. This interface between nationalism and religion inflects the whole nationalist consensus and mediates at a cultural level the social and economic base of Irish nationalism.

However, I would argue that the labour struggles of the urban working class and the attendant espousal of socialism by the labour leaders, was not the only divisive doctrine which the nationalist consensus had to disguise. The social conservatism and Catholicism of the new state felt equally threatened by the British tradition of Protestant liberalism, and the constant resistance of Church and State to any form of social democratic reform was a constant factor in the Ireland of the Thirties,

Forties and Fifties. Again the site of this Protestant liberal tradition was seen to be in the city and the myth of rural self-sufficiency was a potent ideological weapon in the resistance to liberal or social democratic tendencies. In *Strumpet City* this crucial dialectic is also played out in counter-point to the more obvious class antagonisms of the labour struggles.

One of the problems with Irish nationalism is that in cementing the alliance and constructing the consensus, it presented its own dynamics as *intrinsically* Irish and the constructions of Irish culture and history emphasised this uniqueness, this difference. In one sense, this explains the xenophobic nationalism of the Irish Free State and de Valera's Republic and goes some way to understanding the absurdity of "an Irish solution to an Irish problem".

But in reality, Ireland displays a *culturally specific inflection* of movements or ideologies that have been apparent in other developing industrial societies. And crucial to this study of *Strumpet City* is the problematic opposition of the country and the city. What is especially interesting to note is how Irish cultural nationalism mediated this opposition for its own ends, tapping into and moving out of other versions of the same opposition.

Around 1850, Britain reached a crucial watershed in social development — the change from a largely rural society based on agriculture to a largely urban society based on industry. In the United States the significant moment was passed in 1914. In both these countries, dominant cultural attitudes to country and city show significant similarities to the Irish experience.

For example, in 19th century English literature there is a constant attraction to, even nostalgia for, a vanishing, pre-industrial "organic" community, rural in character and traditional in values. This cultural drive is attendant upon the shift to urban industrial society and the assumption to economic power of the urban middle-class. The role of culture is to preserve those values which are being threatened — the organic interdependence of people that supposedly characterised rural society, a closeness to nature and to the soil and, crucially, an adherence to the civilised aesthetic heritage of an aristocracy which is perceived to be in the process of relinquishing political power.[7]

In the novels of George Eliot or Thomas Hardy this central opposition, between rural/traditional society on one hand and urban/modern society on the other, is worked through the narrative and fuels the central dynamic of character and plot. This organicism is an attempt to reconcile the urban/rural divide, to establish traditional values (integration, interdependence, spontaneity) in the seemingly hostile world of urban disintegration and alienation.[8] It is essentially a romantic aesthetic, caught in its own contradiction between a drive for individual expression and a drive for community and harmony. As such it expresses, at the cultural level, the breakdown of a pre-industrial consensus of landowning aristocrats presiding over the contented rural population, and preserving the unity and harmony of the whole through its culture and civilisation. The overarching fear is that the profit-motivated urban middle-class cannot be entrusted to preserve this cultural tradition and that philistinism will result.

In the culture of the United States, the implications of the urban/rural divide are most easily located in the valorisation of western pioneer community which was undertaken, not in the west itself, but in the Eastern cities of New York, Chicago and Boston. The same central contradiction can be located in this cultural project. On the one hand, the need to integrate disparate immigrant cultures into one organic community is juxtaposed with the romantic idealisation of the lone hero/individualist and American culture continues to be pulled between these two poles of populism and individualism.

Even in the utopian socialist writings of the late 19th century, for example, in William Morris' *News from Nowhere,* the socialist society was always seen in terms of a pre-industrial (or more accurately, a post-industrial) organic rural community.

This opposition of country and city was largely seen in biblical terms: the rural serenity of the Garden of Eden was constrasted with the dark satanic mills of the city — heaven and hell.[9]

Returning to the construction of this opposition in Irish culture we can see that the same drives, impulses and romantic overlays are evident, but that the inflections and developments are different. The essential traditional values of rural Ireland have got to be re-established, not because they are under threat from increasing urbanisation as such, but because they have long been under the sulphurous clouds of Britain's satanic mills. There was, therefore, a pressing need to legitimise the concept of an organic, rural culture in Ireland and the cultural nationalist movement stretched back into Gaelic folklore and myth, the Irish language, the adherence of the Irish peasant to the traditional Church and the myth of the individualist, self-sufficient peasant.

The most perfect expression of this drive was in the early and middle poetry of W. B. Yeats. In his romanticisation of the Irish peasant, of mythological heroes and Gaelic folklore, and of the Anglo-Irish Ascendancy, Yeats' disgust of the urban bourgeoisie and the working-class is evident. It is ironic then, that in the 1890's he had attempted to become chief mythologiser of the Catholic nationalist movement but by the 1920's, the victory of the Catholic nationalist bourgeoisie drove him poetically into an acerbic pessimist and politically into the embrace of Irish and European Fascism.[10]

For all their subtle differences, the same anti-urban organicism of Yeats can be located in the writings of other 19th and 20th century writers like Kickham, Somerville and Ross, Lady Gregory and Synge, and in political activists like Arthur Griffith, Michael Collins, Patrick Pearse and Eamon de Valera.

What this has meant in cultural terms for Ireland in the 20th century is the almost total eclipse of the city and the absence of working class struggles from official nationalist history. The nationalist consensus, based on the notion of the historic Irish nation, consolidated an Irish version of the organic community — anti-urban, anti-industrial, historically rural, tenaciously traditional and staunchly Catholic. The visual culture of 20th century Ireland is dominated by romantic images of landscape and idealised images of noble peasants and chaste young maidens. The official culture encouraged sanitised forms of traditional music and Irish dancing and proclaimed the Irish language as the first official language of the state. It encouraged self-sufficiency and self-improvement and built a protective tariff wall around the economy.

Through a rigid system of censorship on books, publications and films it also built a protective cultural wall around the minds of the Irish people. And when these same people took a more materialist view of the rural utopia being constructed, they voted with their feet and left in their millions to the cities of Britain and North America. In 1937, the year in which de Valera's constitution was adopted, the Bishop of Ardagh and Clonmacnoise identified the reason for this un-rural, un-Irish materialism—

> *The emigration of girls to Great Britain: they are lured perhaps by the fascinations of the garish attractions of the city, and by the hectic life of the great world as displayed before their wondering eyes in the glamorous unrealities of the films . . . For it is not the least of the sins of the cinema to breed discontent that is anything but divine in the prosaic placidity of rural life . . .*[11]

Consensus was achieved by containing and making invisible all oppositions, contradictions and alternatives — however, like all consensus, it harnessed the seeds of its own destruction by allowing these contradictions to form a dynamic tension that would pull it asunder. Irish television came into this cultural climate at a time when this nationalist consensus began to break down and for the last two decades has mediated the ideological ruptures that have ensued. A central aspect of these ruptures has been the country/city divide.

The Country and the City in Irish Culture

At its most simple, the country has always been posited as the site of traditional values, peace, harmony and nobility of spirit, whilst the city has characterised disruption, alienation, immorality and barbarism. However this opposition is much more complex. As Raymond Williams explains

> *Most obviously since the Industrial Revolution, but in my view also since the beginnings of the capitalist agrarian mode of production, our powerful images of country and city have been ways of responding to*

a whole social development. This is why, in the end, we must not limit ourselves to their contrast but go on to see their inter-relations and through these the real shape of the underlying crisis.

It is significant, for example, that the common image of the country is now an image of the past, and the common image of the city an image of the future. That leaves, if we isolate them, an undefined present. The pull of the idea of the country is towards old ways, human ways, natural ways. The pull of the idea of the city is towards progress, modernization, development. In what is then a tension, a present experienced as tension, we use the contrast of country and city to ratify an unresolved division and conflict of impulses, which it might be better to face in its own terms. [12] *(my emphasis).*

Strumpet City, although a television adaptation of a literary "classic", is primarily an historical drama serial which marks a significant consummation of nearly two decades of similar endeavour by Irish television to come to terms with the complexities of this tension as outlined by Williams. This endeavour, this process of grappling with a present tension, is what I have referred to earlier as the ideological project of Irish television. In doing so, I am not promoting the idea of a "conspiracy of intent" by individual television producers, or groups of programme makers. However, television entered Irish culture at a moment analagous to the significant point around 1850 in British society — when the divide in rural/urban society was about to shift fundamentally and irrevocably. The cultural turmoil that this caused can now be located in nineteenth century English literature [13] and I would argue that, again, similar aesthetic traumas are evident in Ireland, though inflected in specific ways.

Moreover, because this fundamental shift occurs in Ireland more than a century later, the cultural medium best placed to mediate the ramifications involved was not primarily the novel, but television, itself a product of industrial and technological progress. The different forms and formats that television provided were utilised with varying degrees of success and by looking at some of these, I want to suggest ways of understanding the nature of this ideological project.

The Serial — *Tolka Row*

At its most simplistic, a culture that had posited a fairly unproblematic ideology of rural utopia as the basis of its consensus was badly in need of counter-pointing images of urban society. Dashing the hopes and confirming the fears of traditionalists, television, by its very nature, was to prove incapable of blandly supporting a consensus that was itself being undermined by new economic strategies anyway. Television needs drama (across all of its functions and formats, including news and information) and drama needs conflict. The slow disintegration of this consensus provided conflict in plenty.

In 1963, Telefís Éireann (as it then was) brought to the screen an urban drama serial called *Tolka Row*. The serial was based in a Dublin working class community, concentrating largely on two families, the Nolans and the Feeneys, but bringing in a range of other characters to provide the necessary interaction of personal, private and public conflict. The serial did have models to look to, especially, of course, *Coronation Street* on British television, which was into its third year by this stage, and *Tolka Row* was very much an attempt at an Irish version of the British serial. *Tolka Row* ran for five years and was dropped in 1968, by which time the rural serial *The Riordans* had established itself as RTE's most popular programme. *Tolka Row* has now drifted into the realms of folk memory for older Irish television viewers and only the final episode is available for study today.[14] During its five year run though it was extremely popular, but under competition from *The Riordans* (both in terms of limited drama budget and viewers' affections) its decline was rapid. One of the *Tolka Row* scriptwriters, Wesley Burrowes, later the main writer of *The Riordans,* gave his own reasons for its decline:

> I believe that the eternal family bickering among the Nolans and the Feeneys eventually killed *Tolka Row*. . . .[15]

Tolka Row was produced to provide an outlet for the largely unheard voice of working class Dublin. It was, in many ways, the beginning of Irish television's project to re-insert this missing discourse of the city into Irish culture and perhaps this is why it ultimately failed. If Burrowes is correct, then, ideologically, *Tolka Row* only re-confirmed the simplistic notion of city life implicit in rural mythologies. The city is the site of disharmony and communal breakdown. Whatever the intentions may have been, it was no good throwing out city images simply because, in themselves, they provided oppositional culture that would therefore create some desired frisson in the real world. As Luke Gibbons argues elsewhere in this volume, if the thesis was the myth of rural harmony, then it is much more effective to undermine that myth from within, i.e. in the context of the rural serial, and *The Riordans* was ideally placed to do this.

I want now to look more closely at the final episode of *Tolka Row* and try to suggest the basic contradiction at the heart of a strategy designed to provide for the first time in Irish culture positive sympathetic images of the working class. By extension, it becomes clearer that television tried to insert a specific version of the absent discourse of the city and one that leads ultimately to *Strumpet City*.

The dramatic and ideological centre of the Tolka Row community is the Nolan family — Jack and Rita, their son Sean, their daughter Peggy, now married to Andy Kinnear. The Nolans are the dependable, stable working class family, good neighbours, sympathetic listeners and purveyors of good advice. In her marriage to Andy, Peggy has extended the family to include a new source of communal dependability and her pregnancy augurs well for the continuing stability of this community.

The Nolans are used to counterpoint the other characters — the nosey gossip, Philo Feeney, the lazy and indolent Chas and Queenie Butler, the neurotic and slightly pathetic Statia Doyle and the "bit of a chancer" Gerry O'Reilly. The generational problems pursued through the Nolans' son Sean and their lodger, Michael Carney, also counterpoint their stability. (Peggy's pregnancy, though wrapped in the chaste embrace of holy wedlock is an important ideological intrusion into a culture that had once deemed the birth scene in *Gone With The Wind* too explicit for the rural simplicity of Ireland in the Forties.[16])

And yet here is the problem. The community represented by the Nolans is also an idealisation, required in the first instance as a dramatic convention of the serial form, but also tapping directly into the rural myth of community stability. As Raymond Williams points out in the above quote, there is a greater interrelatedness between the city and rural mythologies than a simplistic opposition credits, and the existence of, and need for, communal stability is as much a part of city life as it is the rural. But Ireland was a society that developed on precisely such a simplistic opposition so the idealisation of the Nolan family is perceived through the existing rural mythologies. The Nolans *are* a rural ideal so that any counter-pointing is ultimately going to re-inforce rural prejudices.

In this episode of *Tolka row,* for example, Chas and Queenie Butler are compulsive petty gamblers — ("Ah, Chas, there's bingo tonight"). They are heavily in debt, as a result ("There goes the HP money") and liable to drift into petty crime (Chas' agreement to handles the "hot" watches for the seedy Gerry O'Reilly). Whilst trying to present working class culture positively and sympathetically, *Tolka Row* ends up confirming at least some rural prejudices — the city is the site of petty crime, petty gambling, laziness and unemployment, those characteristics of Chas and Queenie.

The internal squabblings of families, especially if it includes the Nolans, will only re-inforce further that city life is intrinsically incapable of supporting stable community. And finally, if *Tolka Row* is to raise issues so far deemed taboo (like the sexual politics hinted at in Peggy's pregnancy, or in the younger characters' social life) they will also be seen as intrinsic to the city and their effect thus diminished.

The operation of this problem can be seen in the way in which one of the sub-plots is finally closed. Gabby Doyle and his wife Statia are leaving Tolka Row and returning to Gabby's home in Donegal. Gabby is delighted to be moving — "Ah, but it'll be great to be back in the green hills of Donegal" he says. To emphasise the essential rural aspect of Gabby's character, he is framed lighting his pipe by the mantlepiece, above which hangs a cheap reproduction of a typically romantic landscape painting. The combination of pipe, connoting peace and personal satisfaction, and landscape, connoting all the harmonious aspects of nature, reinforces that Gabby's decision is to give up a losing battle to find peace and community in the hostile environs of the city.

Gabby's wife, Statia, is a Dubliner, and part of the Doyles' drama in this episode is the fact that she is actually leaving home in the city to go to Donegal. Obviously this involves yielding to her husband's wishes on one hand and parting with a way of life that she grew up in on the other hand. Her obvious sadness and reluctance is in marked contrast to Gabby's enthusiasm. However, the rest of the community rallies to support Gabby's decision and assure Statia. In the end, there is general agreement that it is all for the best — rural retreat is the obvious answer even for the city-bred Statia, and if the audience might harbour lingering doubts about Statia's ability to adapt to Donegal, the thrust of the narrative is towards reassurance for Statia and audience alike. The struggle is over, and rural tranquility beckons.

Tolka Row looked at city life *from the perspective of the country ideal,* in an attempt to posit a progressive opposition to dominant representations. However the issues it raised, the dramatic devices it used, indeed the very form of the serial itself conspired to turn its progressive intent against itself. A much more successful project was to turn the perspective of the city onto the country through the conventions of a rural serial, as in *The Riordans* and, as Luke Gibbons again argues, this explains the unique contribution of *The Riordans.*

Dominant rural mythologies, in the cultural ferment of contemporary Ireland, will not readily disappear because dialectical oppositions are posed against them. When the very act of seeing and comprehending are already imbued with rural ideologies, the more pressing need is to enter into the rural myths and unravel them internally.

With apologies for historical anachronism, I think it is fair to say that *Coronation Street* would not have worked either in the Britain of the 1850's. This raises the whole question of *historical and social conjuncture,* i.e., the precise moment and historical conditions in which culture is produced. Thus the novel in 19th century England shows the ideological resonances of that particular conjuncture, running below and through the level of plot and character. In the same way, in the Ireland of the 1960's, when the economy was being modernised and the social structures opened out to wider influences, it is only to be expected that the culture being produced, in this case television drama, would also display the resonances of this particular conjuncture. It was the complexities of this conjuncture which defeated *Tolka Row* and it was the complexities of this conjuncture which gave the programme its ideological gloss.

Tolka Row was an attempt at re-inserting the missing discourse of the urban working class into Irish culture and as such, can be seen as an important element in television's wider ideological project — providing cultural support for the modernising impulses of the economy at large. However, the final episode of the serial also illuminates the particular inflection which this larger project was to take. The dramatic centre is, again, the Nolan family.

It had been decided to drop *Tolka Row* at the end of the 1968 season so in advance the script had to begin the process of closing down all plots and sub-plots. The serial form works out from the permanence of a central family/community group and it is not surprising that the device used to bring permanent closure to the serial was the breaking up of this central community. The Nolans are forced into emigration, literally to Coventry, where Jack has secured a steady, well-paid job. The central drama of the last episode is the trauma of this move as felt most specifically by the community mother-figure, Rita Nolan.

The structure of the scene in which Jack and Rita discuss their move to Coventry emphasises the catastrophic effect this will have on the whole community. The scene opens with a shot of the Nolan's front door, cuts to a close-up of a ticking clock beside the delph on their kitchen cupboard, cuts again to a large close-up of a tea-pot, as we hear Jack and Rita reminiscing about some good times they have had and some of Peggy's old boyfriends, and cuts finally to Jack and Rita who are revealed washing dishes as they talk. The rest of their conversation is counter-pointed with the loud sound of the ticking clock.

The editing emphasises the iconography of home and community, especially the tea-pot which symbolises the great reliever of personal problems. Indeed in all serials, and especially in *The Riordans,* the combination of mother figure and tea-pot is the absolute assurance of community comfort, understanding and support.

The Nolan's conversation turns to the problem of emigration juxtaposing their personal experience, ("We'll be back, Rita. Our roots are here" —) with the greater social problem — ("It's the Irish curse . . . I was reading somewhere that over one million people have left Ireland since 1940. Not many of them came back.")

Rita then asks Jack if there is any answer to the problem.

Rita: Have you ever asked yourself Jack . . .?
Jack: Yes, Rita, often, but I don't have an answer. Maybe them politicians have, but I haven't.

Jacks ends the conversation by stating that there is no hope for his generation but that maybe there is hope for Sean and his generation.

The scene underscores the basic premise that when the centre of the community is destroyed, the whole community support system collapses. Rita worries throughout the programme about whether or not Sean and Michael will be able to look after themselves when she has gone and at various points Mrs. Feeney, Maggie Bonar and Jack all reassure her that they will be alright. The representation of Rita Nolan as community mother figure, whose task is to support the home, look after her husband and, most crucially, take care of her unmarried son, is important for understanding the wider implications of the scene described above.

As the conversation moves into the greater social reality of unemployment and emigration, Rita — as community mother-figure for Tolka Row — enlarges to become Rita as Mother Ireland herself, that most resonant of Irish female symbols. And when Jack responds by referring to "them politicians", the implication becomes clear. The community needs a larger support system from the State in order to maintain its caring centre.

The ideological ramifications for Ireland of such a suggestion are immense. For what is being raised here is that other aspect of the city which the Nationalist and Catholic consensus had effectively disguised for forty years — the impulses of the British Protestant liberal and social democratic tradition. The Catholic Church in Ireland constantly opposed any suggestion of State interference in social or family matters and indeed the hierarchy brought about the collapse of the government in 1951 because of its refusal to endorse the "Mother and Child" scheme, a proposal to offer state support to mothers in the home. It was condemned vitriolically from the pulpits as an unwarranted intrusion on the sanctity of the Irish family.

A generation later, *Tolka Row* is implicitly condemning the State for its failure to provide just such a support system, bringing attention to its failure to develop the necessary social democratic mechanisms that would keep Rita Nolan within her community. Despite the myths of "frugal self-sufficiency" and intrinsic rural virtues, Mother Ireland needs the type of English welfarism that the nationalist consensus had always denied. As the Nolans wash the dishes for the last time in the security of their own kitchen, time ticks away (or is that a time-bomb which is heard above their conversation?)

This reading of *Tolka Row* does, I think, give a clear indication of the wider ideological project of Irish television over the last two decades. This project is essentially liberal in nature and committed to the development of a more caring society through a comprehensive welfare state system. In *Tolka Row* we can see a glimpse of this project — it is much more explicit in the *Late Late Show* (see Maurice Earls below) and in the structures of various current affairs programmes (see Mary Kelly below).

The Single Play — *A Week In The Life Of Martin Cluxton*

We can locate it as well in RTE's single-plays which have attempted to deal with urban issues and I want to look briefly at one of the earliest and most successful examples of these — *A Week In The Life Of Martin Cluxton* from December 1971. The play, which was written, produced and directed by Brian MacLochlain, who also produced the final episode of *Tolka Row,* follows the first week back in Dublin of teenager Martin Cluxton, who has just returned from over two years in Borstal for "robbing from cars".

The dramatic device of the play is to blend its fictional material into a documentary mould in the tradition of British television drama of the 1960's.[17] This drive towards documentary is only thinly disguised as fiction. The particular reform school featured is called "Glenmulken" and is obviously based on the real reform school at Letterfrack, in Connemara, which was used up until the early 70's as a depository for mainly Dublin young offenders. The reality of Letterfrack is, in itself, a potent example of the simplistic division of country/city myths that permeated the nationalist consensus for forty years.

These young city children, the victims of the city's alienating and hostile environment, were sent to Letterfrack and put through a harsh discipline in the harsh beauty of Connemara. This discipline, devised and supervised by the Irish Christian Brothers, included all the elements one would expect — a strong, authoritarian regime, mingled with a strongly Catholic morality, including respect for law and order and private property, and an inculcation into the beauties and traditions of the "real" Ireland, the Connemara Gaeltacht.

In a flash-back sequence, Martin Cluxton remembers his first day in Glenmulken. The Christian Brother begins the lesson with some prayers in Irish and then goes on to talk about the need for law and order, using the example of nature's laws and disciplines evident all around them in Connemara.

The play operates immediately to highlight the absurdity of this short, shock treatment in rural Ireland as an answer to urban problems. Thus Martin's progress back into his city environment, with its attendant problems of poverty, over-crowding and lack of opportunity, leads inevitably back to petty crime.

However, the play's drive towards documentary realism, implicit in its use of locations in the streets and flat complexes of inner Dublin, is reinforced by a series of direct-to-camera addresses by the various figures of authority — the Christian Brother in Glenmulken, two St. Vincent de Paul brothers and the Parish Priest in Martin's Dublin home.

These direct addresses, by the actors playing the roles, form the ideological centre of the play. Significantly, they are all representatives of Catholic Church authority and they all emphasise the same points. The Christian Brother, for instance, speaking right at the beginning of the play, declares — "We are neither qualified nor equipped to carry out the work of rehabilitation" — and framed as he is against the mountains and heather of Connemara, the audience feels that this is probably true. The St. Vincent de Paul brothers, addressing the audience from their car, claim that they are being asked to perform the functions of social worker, marriage guidance counsellor, psychologist, even family planning adviser, none of which they are qualified to do. Finally, the parish priest, touring the problem families in the flat complex, note-book in hand, can only offer Martin the prospect of healthy pursuits in the local youth club. In his address to camera, he describes Martin's problems as threefold —medical, environmental and spiritual. He can help spiritually, he declares, but cannot help with medical or environmental problems.

Throughout the play, then, what is being highlighted is the lack of professional state-funded support systems, again the social democratic structures which would alleviate the problems. Significantly, those support systems which do exist, Catholic charities or Catholic religious orders, are declaring that they are now inadequate to the task and are actively calling for just such support systems which the Church rejected in the Mother-and-Child scheme of 1951.

To re-emphasise its liberal/social democratic message, the play uses two other characters, mouth-pieces for different types of oppositional practice, both of them trailing the traces of the play's late sixties ambience.

On his mother's instructions, Martin goes to the pub to try and retrieve his unemployed father, and finds him in conversation with a combat-jacketted political activist (whom the credits identify as "Maoist"). This character mouths a series of left-wing platitudes about the working class mobilising to improve its own lot and if the words "running-dog lackeys of Imperialism" are not used exactly, the implications are clear enough. This empty rhetoric only helps to underline the inability of this one worker to organise himself out of the pub and home to his suffering family.

The second mouth-piece is the philosopher tramp that Martin encounters on the beaches of Dublin Bay. This tramp, obviously educated, has chosen the sixties option of dropping out and living off "the waste of the good people of Dublin". Whilst this character is, like the Maoist, very much a product of the late Sixties, the oppositional position to the city which he occupies has a more general reference. The use, here, of the natural landscape of Dublin Bay has interesting similarities to the way this is used in *Strumpet City,* as I discuss later, and its force is none other than to posit the uncomplicated opposition of city and country. The tramp, however, confirms that dropping out of the city, a society he condemns as being built on waste, is not an option for Martin Cluxton, and anyway, the audience already knows that Martin's enforced drop-out to the natural splendours of Glenmulken has done nothing to improve his prospects.

In this, I feel that *A Week In The Life Of Martin Cluxton* is a significant advance on *Tolka Row.* The play brings into dramatic conflict the rural/urban divide and by doing so, avoids the trap which *Tolka Row* fell into. By totally excluding the rural, by leaving it, as it were, outside and unchallenged, the serial, despite itself, allowed the potency of rural myths to undermine its progressive intent. By including the rural discourse, I think *Martin Cluxton* comes closer to Raymond Williams concept of "the present experienced as tension" and comes closer to the social reality of contemporary Ireland where the transition of the economy has created a more complex interrelation of the urban and rural discourse, in effect an ideology in flux.

In the end, therefore, *A Week In The Life Of Martin Cluxton* rejects Catholic charity, socialist organisation and rural escape as solutions to the problems of contemporary urban society. In doing so, it calls for the development of a caring welfare state, reinforcing the message of *Tolka Row* and anticipating the message of *Strumpet City*.

Ideology In Flux — *Strumpet City*

In relation to RTE programmes over the last two decades, I have been arguing a number of points.

1. Analysis of RTE programmes reveals a general ideological project.
2. This project can be summarised as the insertion into Irish culture of discourses rendered invisible by the nationalist consensus of the twenties to the sixties.
3. The particular inflection that this insertion took was essentially liberal and social democratic.
4. In the case of the urban serial, a combination of historical conjuncture and formal conventions conspired to turn its progressive intent against itself.

If we now look at *Strumpet City* in this light, I think it becomes easier to place its importance more precisely. For convenience I will look at the programme under a number of different headings but, as will be seen, the issues raised intertwine throughout in a more complex weave than the headings might suggest.

(i) *Strumpet City* as Television History

The first distinguishing element of *Strumpet City* is that it is television historical drama, or costume drama to use the slightly pejorative name for the genre. This raises some important formal issues about the role and structure of narrative and the conception of history implicit in dominant television practices.

The most sustained analysis of history on television is by Colin McArthur[18] and I think it is worth examining some of McArthur's conclusions for relevance to *Strumpet City*. This by extension will raise a more theoretical issue concerning analysis of television in Ireland, for it will mean testing the theoretical conclusions of analysis undertaken in one context, that of Britain, and applying it to another, that of Ireland.

McArthur analyses a variety of British television programmes about history, both drama and documentary, and locates six characteristics of what he calls the dominant conception of history:

(a) a belief in the uniqueness of the event;

(b) a belief in the free-will and moral responsibility of the individual;

(c) a belief in the role of historical accident (or more precisely, there is no conception of structural explanations of events);

(d) a strong reliance on the role and testimony of individuals (particularly "great" men);

(e) a strong concern with the nation state, both in its political and military dimensions;

(f) a belief in progress and in "chronological monism" — i.e., the steady movement forward from one isolated time to another with a simple cause and effect dynamic.

These characteristics are a result of two factors. Firstly, the demands of narrative for character identification tend to emphasise the role of individuals at the expense of structures and institutions and secondly the demands of narrative for a linear progression leading towards resolution and closure tends to deny the more complex dialectical movement of history.[19]

The validity of McArthur's analysis would seem to be borne out by the fact that historiography, and the teaching of history even at second level education, has moved a long way from these simplistic approaches. Social and economic history has long come to terms with deeper underlying structures, like modes of production, class conflict, social institutions and conceptual relationships between different periods of history.[20] Television history, especially but not exclusively historical drama, still plucks out great men (occasionally women) and great events, like Henry VIII, the Churchills, Lloyd George, or the Boer War, the Great War and the General Strike.

Robert Kee's series *Ireland – A Television History* was a recent example of all of these characteristics. Each of its thirteen episodes gave a straightforward chronological account of Ireland through its great men and great events, dramatising some sections for identification purposes (most notoriously in the episode on Parnell) and mediating the rest through that other great man, Mr. Kee himself, largely through on-camera narrative. Robert Kee is a much more complex historian than this series would suggest[21] and one must assume that he anticipates the need for a scapegoat in the title of the series itself — *A Television History*.

McArthur, however, goes on to argue that television drama can indeed deal with more complex approaches to history, especially when it jettisons some of the most constricting conventions of narrative.[22] Elsewhere, he makes a persuasive case for the use of juxtaposition within fairly conventional narrative[23] and this he calls "progressive realism". By approaching *Strumpet City* as progressive realism, I think one can assess how successful it is, within straightforward narrative, in presenting a more complex conception of history.

It must first be admitted though, that *Strumpet City* displays, superficially at least, some of the characteristics outlined by McArthur.

Most obviously, by the casting of Peter O'Toole as Jim Larkin, the programme re-inforces the historical importance of the "great man", bringing the full force of the star-system and its attendant connotations[24] into play. Indeed, throughout the seven episodes, there is constant reference to "Larkin's Union" and "the boul' Jim Larkin". The programme conspires in reproducing the dominant historical view of Larkin as an incredibly charismatic leader who was held in near-reverence by the workers and viewed with singular odium by the bosses and who single-handedly created the labour crises of 1913.

Another aspect of the programme is that its array of colourful and likeable characters are mobilised to achieve maximum emotional impact through audience identification. The importance of this kind of emotional response explains why there are seven episodes, rather than the more usual four or six. When it was first screened, episodes one and two were screened together on the first evening, allowing time in episode one to introduce the main characters and fill in their personalities and problems. By the time episode two was over, it was hoped that audiences would care enough about this disparate group of individuals to tune in the following week. This was a programme strategy which was utilised most recently by Granada's production of *The Jewel In The Crown* and, to move from the sublime to the ridiculous, by the BBC programming of the American import *The Thorn Birds.*

Indeed, *Strumpet City* lays itself open to the charge that it is historical soap-opera by also employing the devices of soap-opera to bridge commercial breaks and ease transition from one episode to another —i.e., a reliance on a series of emotional highpoints and climaxes.

Finally, it could also be argued that, despite its historical span of seven years, the programme isolates one set of circumstances and follows them through a relentless progression of narrative details to an inevitable closure. The emphasis on character furthermore offers the conclusion that this inevitability can be traced back to specific decisions by specific individuals, possibly the result of individual character faults, and thus denying the more complex dynamics of economics, social institutions and class conflicts.

Let us begin, therefore, the process of assessing *Strumpet City*'s conception of history, and its implied ideological meaning, and I want to begin by considering first of all the question of characterisation.

(ii) *Characterisation*

> *There is nothing of the satirist, no bitterness in this writer's composition. As a result, one leaves the book down with something of the same sensation with which one ended* Dr Zhivago, *with a renewed faith in the essential decency of people, if only they could escape from the snares of the human condition.*[25]

This quote from Terence de Vere White's review of the original novel highlights the importance of *Strumpet City*'s gallery of characters and the traditional literary response to them. If we look, for example, at the main characters in the plot, this essential decency is evident.

Rashers Tierney is a city tramp, whose *essential* human qualities of good-humour, kindness, compassion and friendship shine through the coarseness of his appearance and the hardship of his poverty. Barney Mulhall is a militant trade-unionist whose *essential* human qualities of justice, fellowship, concern and dedication shine through the bullishness of his political commitment. Mary is a young mother whose *essential* human qualities of maternal instinct, good neighbourliness, generosity and selflessness shine through her ambitious drive to improve herself. And Mr. Yearling is an employer whose *essential* human qualities of sense of duty, charity, love of children and love of culture shine through the detached cynicism of his privileged status. And so on.

Each character has a specific fault, or set of faults, but in reality is a decent caring human being caught up in a situation which he/she did not create. This extreme rigidity of characterisation, implicit in Plunkett's original novel (and arguably a basic structural convention of all novels) is retained in Hugh Leonard's adaptation for television. But I think there is a deeper set of structural relationships between the characters than even this suggests.

If the main characters are broken down into their obvious general categories we get a typology like this —

Working Class	*Clergy*	*Ruling Class*
Bob Fitzpatrick (Fitz)	Fr. Giffley	Ralph Bradshaw
Mary Fitzpatrick	Fr. O'Connor	Florence Bradshaw
Barney Mulhall	Fr. O'Sullivan	Belton Yearling
Pat Bannister		
Miss Gilchrist		
Lily Maxwell		
"Toucher" Hennessy		
Rashers Tierney		

Jim Larkin is a presence that exists outside and above the rest, his special status again reinforced by the special status of the Hollywood superstar, Peter O'Toole, but also by the fact that his infrequent appearances receive a build up through constant reference and report by the other characters.

Immediately, we can see that the great number of working class characters emphasises *Strumpet City*'s greater interest in and sympathy for the working class. But such a bald categorization disguises the complex set of interconnections between the characters, running horizontally across the categories and vertically within them. The interplay between the characters is so complex that some of them connect across or down through more than one movement.

The combination of internal hierarchy and plot for example would locate Mary and Miss Gilchrist within the ruling class milieu, albeit in a subservient capacity, downstairs in the kitchen. The plot moves to connect Mary to the inner-city community through her marriage to Fitz and Miss Gilchrist is removed to the workhouse. However, this classic "upstairs, downstairs" hierarchy is also to be found within the category of the working class. This hierarchy could be categorized in the following way —

Honest Workers
The Fitzpatricks
The Mulhalls
(The Farrells)
Pat
Miss Gilchrist — servant in Kingstown

Marginal Workers
Hennessy (work shy)
Lily Maxwell (prostitute)

Lumpen Proletariat
Rashers Tierney (city tramp)

Thus this hierarchy is supported by Rashers' lumpen proletariat position in the basement and moves upwards through the marginal worker status of the work-shy Hennessy to the higher status of the honest workers Pat, Mulhall and Fitz. There is actual and implied movement up and down this hierarchy. Miss Gilchrist, for example, who is an honest worker until old age makes her no longer employable as the Bradshaws' servant, is thrown out to the work-house and dies on the same social level that Rashers does. Perhaps the depth of this level is symbolised by the fact that Rashers' rotting corpse is discovered beside that of his dog and even if Fr. O'Connor can distinguish between the brute beast and the immortal soul, all three, Rashers, Miss Gilchrist and the dog, end up as decaying and discarded flesh.

In the sense of implied movement, obviously *any* of the honest workers could move down to marginal or lumpen status and the effects of the long lock-out achieve this to some extent. However, Lily moves up from marginal status (prostitute) to honest worker (gutting and selling fish) and presumably to Mary's status of mother by her marriage to Pat.

The dynamic of hierarchy, plot and implied movement operates as well in relation to the clergy. In episode six, Fr. Giffley confirms that he once enjoyed the same kind of literate and cultured company that Fr. O'Connor now does, that he was sent originally to the slum parish of St. Brigid's "to take me down a peg or two" but that his descent was even greater than that. In his alcoholic madness at the end, Fr. Giffley occupies a clerical basement every bit as lowly as Rashers' proletarian one. This downward flow of the narrative leaves Rashers, his dog, Miss Gilchrist and Fr. Giffley occupying the same status as ultimate victims.

Fr. O'Sullivan, on the other hand is portrayed as the clergy version of the honest worker whose simple humanity and affinity to the workers is emphasised by his closeness to the Mulhall family. Operating the logic of implied movement, it becomes obvious that Fr. O'Sullivan's choice of clergy status is all that has saved him from worker status with its attendant dangers of further decline.

I think now we can see that these connections across and down the original categories begin to take on symbolic resonances. This can be shown if we isolate a number of connections along lines designated by similar character traits. For example, love of children as a basic trait would unite Mary, who is in the process of having too many, with Mrs. Bradshaw and Yearling, who compensate for not having any in different ways. Mrs. Bradshaw offers up the small sacrifice of not eating meat on Wednesdays and holds children's parties on Corpus Christi. Yearling's compensation is shown by his admiration for the young girl playing by the pond, his generosity to the young boy climbing the tree, to whom he gives a shilling and finally when he goes to the slums to help escort the starving children to the boats.

Love of music as a character trait produces the surprising connection of Rashers to Fr. O'Connor, Yearling and the Bradshaws. Rashers' humble tin whistle and pieces of instant doggerel connect across to Yearling's cello, Mrs. Bradshaw's piano and Fr. O'Connor's tenor voice. On another line of connection, Mulhall's dogged commitment to socialism echoes Fr. O'Connor's dogged adherence to fundamental catholicism which in turn relates to Bradshaw's dogged defence of class privilege.

The rigidity, then, of the class positions outlined in the broad categories earlier now looks extremely complex when interconnections are made across movements and relationships real, implied and symbolic. In a broad movement across all the characters, a view of general humanity is proposed, an essentially humanist perspective that would seem to imply that the tragedy of the Dublin working class is the tragedy of all humanity. Under the umbrella of humanity, class oppression is contained and disguised and what we are left with is, in de Vere White's phrase, "the snares of the human condition".

We are now back in the familiar territory of consensus — exactly this process of containment and disguise of contradictions which I located originally in the nationalist consensus in Ireland. However, it is important to distinguish between the process (containment and disguise) and the nature of the consensus itself and to clarify what is being constructed ideologically in this reading of *Strumpet City,* we can isolate and examine more closely some of these lines of inter-connection.

One aspect of the characterisation of *Strumpet City* which we have seen is that despite the attempts of the narrative to identify the main protagonists as real, human people, the thrust towards a general humanity actually forces the individuality of each to collapse into a pattern of stereotypes. This is seen in its most classic form in the stereotyping of the main women characters where Mary is portrayed at the beginning as the chaste rural maiden (the virgin) and through marriage to Fitz becomes the loving caring mother (Mary — virgin —mother). Lily, on the other hand, is the woman of the city streets, the proverbial prostitute with the heart of gold, who slips into the dangerous depths by contracting a venereal disease and threatens to end up her own version of decaying and discarded flesh. However, through her own determination and the prospect of marriage to Pat, her decline is arrested, and she is one of the few characters at the end who displays any hope for the future.

The ideological weight of the stereotyping of Mary is obvious — however Lily's more classic portrayal as a prostitute has further resonances. Lily, in fact, symbolises the strumpet herself, the City, and the old nationalist myth of Dublin as the city prostituted to the English is underscored by her having a portrait of Queen Victoria on her wall. The more peripheral women characters, Miss Gilchrist, the servant and Mrs. Bradshaw, her ruling class superior, are both childless (as are the other characters of the ruling class milieu, Bradshaw, Yearling and the celibate O'Connor). However, the general stereotype of women as natural mothers, emphasised by Yearling in relation to the little girl by the pond (whom he identifies as Cathleen Ní Houlihan, no less — Mother Ireland herself) is applicable to both of them and ties into the larger discourse of care and love of children which is at the centre of the narrative. This obviously leads to the confrontation at the dockside when the slum children are being led to the boat, but the whole play on children is emphasised throughout the seven episodes by another stereotypical device. All scenes in the working class slums are established by the convention of showing children playing on the streets and on the stairs of the slum tenements or by the sound of babies crying in the background. However, before pursuing further the implications of the women characters it is important to consider how the use of stereotypes applies to the male characters as well.

We have already seen how the character trait of stubborn dogmatism links Mulhall, Fr. O'Connor and Bradshaw. Just as the stereotyping of Mary and Lily actually lends symbolic weight to their ideological roles the character trait here imbues the male characters with the force of ideological representatives. Thus Mulhall is the mouthpiece of militant socialism, Fr. O'Connor of fundamental Catholicism and Bradshaw of bourgeois privilege. In the interaction of these three characters a consistent pattern of confrontation and identification takes place.

Both Mulhall and Fr. O'Connor provide the dramatic moments of confrontation. In episode five, for example, Mulhall goes to Fr. O' Connor and confronts him with the issue of parochial relief parcels being denied to the families of strikers. The result is not compromise, but Mulhall's physical assault on Fr. O'Connor's relief worker, Keever. Interestingly, the move from confrontation to physical violence is also an aspect of the priest's commitment when he leads the hymn-singing Catholics against those escorting the children to the boats.

Mulhall's politics, of course, put him in a confrontation with the ruling class so, although, as characters, they never meet, Mulhall is diametrically opposed to Bradshaw. Fr. O'Connor and Bradshaw, through their friendship, class position and religion are in close alliance.

As mouthpieces for ideological positions therefore, the links between Mulhall, Fr. O'Connor and Bradshaw produces a confrontation that can be characterised as —

Socialism ⟶ *confrontation* ⟶ Fundamental Catholicism
Bourgeois Privilege

Two points can be made about this "ideological map". Firstly, its mouthpieces do not move position at all from start to finish. Mulhall, Fr. O'Connor and Bradshaw remain consistent in their views, unbending and unrepentant. The confrontation is a struggle for complete power and domination. Secondly, the implications of this ideological stand-off are pursued through the symbolic presence of children and this is where the rather regressive stereotyping of the women characters solely as mothers and victims is important. In the women characters most closely identified with this stereotype, the male ideologies are seen to have the most profound effect.

Mary, the innocent victim/mother suffers when Fitz goes on strike and in this she symbolises the plight of all the working-class mothers. However, she also has to cope with Fr. O'Connor's fundamental zeal when he investigates the rumour that she is to send her children to England. In Mary's absence, he insults her and chides her for giving her money to Mrs. Mulhall. The unmaterialist lack of concern that his philosophy implies is articulated when he declares in the final episode —

> *"When the souls of young children are at stake, there are worse things than a pauper's grave."*

Mrs. Bradshaw inhabits the childless world of upper class privilege, and the many manifestations of her "natural maternal feelings" receive constant chiding and insult from her husband. In this clash of "male" ideologies, women and children are presented as the main victims, literally squeezed in the middle.

                    confrontation   Fundamental Catholicism
Socialism ⟵——— Women/children ⟶ Bourgeois privilege

The role then of the other two main male characters, Fitz and

Yearling, is crucial. If we examine their respective relationships to characters within and across the general categories outlined earlier, a consistent pattern of compromise and movement emerges, in contrast to the sterile dogmatism of the ideological mouth-pieces.

Fitz, for example, in episode six is more sympathetic to the plight of the marginal worker, Hennessy, than Mulhall's hard line attitude will allow for. Although he agrees to talk Hennessy out of continuing as a night watchman he appeals not to have him beaten up as a scab, which is Mulhall's solution to the problem. Again, he is promoted to foreman in Morgan's foundry and the obvious pride he takes in his upward mobility echoes Mary's drive towards self-improvement.

When the employers bring about the final confrontation over union membership, Fitz, as an honest worker and good trade-unionist, walks out with the other men. However, before doing so, he stays long enough to train the office-staff how to reduce the furnace heat slowly, thus avoiding damage. A small compromise, certainly, but a characteristic of Fitz which Mulhall patently lacks. More importantly, though, is his relationship to the clergy.

At the beginning of episode four, Fr. O'Connor is attending a workers' meeting for the release of the imprisoned Larkin. The platform speaker echoes the confrontation at its most stark when he declares — "The employers, the police and the clergy are our enemies". The ensuing cheers and applause from his assembled parishioners visibly upsets the worried priest. Fitz, however, has noticed his distress and comes to his aid, offering his arm for support as he leads him away from the meeting. To underline Fitz's ability to compromise, there is a similar scene in episode six. Again, he lends a supporting arm to the drunken Fr. Giffley as he leads him out of the pub to a waiting carriage. It is no surprise then, that when Rashers' decaying body is discovered in the basement, it is Fitz who is there to join in the prayers as Fr. O'Connor officiates over last rites.

There is a similar tendency to compromise, with more pronounced movement from his original position, in Yearling and his dealings with his original allies, Bradshaw and Fr. O'Connor. Yearling's growing disillusionment with Bradshaw manifests itself in a detached cynicism. In episode one, he talks about the upper class values of gentility and manners, dismissing them as a kind of game invented by the English, who will therefore always play the game better. Having lost at this game once, because of his Irish attachment to whiskey, Yearling clearly drifts into the same kind of loss of faith that leads Fr. Giffley to alcoholism. However, through his love for children, Yearling's detachment is gradually replaced by concern and finally commitment.

At the Corpus Christi garden party for children, he attacks Bradshaw directly over the condition of the slums which he rents to Dublin's poor, warning him of the consequences should they collapse. When this inevitable catastrophe happens, with heavy loss of life, Yearling has nothing but contempt for Bradshaw and disdain for Fr. O'Connor's sympathy towards the slum land-lord's ensuing difficulties. Finally, the plight of the starving children spurs him to action and he agrees to help escort them to the boats that will carry them to workers' families in England. As he walks with them, he recites another children's rhyme, linking back to the previous occasion he did so, as he pondered the significance of the little girl by the pond. On that occasion, he likened the girl to Cathleen Ní Houlihan herself, and now, as he walks with the city's children to the boat, Yearling is symbolically helping the young Ireland in her hour of need.

In his relationships with Fr. O'Connor, Yearling displays the same movement away from his previous position. Throughout, he plays a theological game with Fr. O'Connor's dogmatic faith, sometimes, as in episode one, chiding the priest from his agnostic position and wittily, though pointedly, attacking Catholicism's most blatant absurdities, as he sees them. Gradually, he begins to distance himself from Fr. O'Connor's inability to face up to the material realities of this world, especially over Bradshaw's crimes as a slum landlord. The final estrangement is a violent and bloody one.

The proposals to remove Dublin's starving children to the families of workers in England was an important show of solidarity between Irish and English workers. The Church's response, however, was prompt, predictable and effective. Since, in all likelihood, these English families would be Protestant, the Church condemned the proposal as an attempt to sacrifice the immortal souls of young children, in order to nourish their bodily health.[26]

In episode six, Fr. O'Sullivan regrets the displacement of families that this would involve, but is prepared to acknowledge that it might be necessary to save the children from further starvation. Fr. O'Connor can countenance no such compromise and immediately declares that such a move will be stopped "with force, if necessary". So when Yearling joins the group of middle-class intellectuals helping to escort the children, he confronts the Church militant in its most stark form.

In the ensuing scramble, he is beaten unconscious and only escapes further violence by Fr. O'Connor's intervention. This marks the end of their friendship — "Call off your hymn-chanting thugs". At this point, Yearling has developed from a position of detached class privilege to one of intense liberal and humanist concern and in doing so, he comes to occupy an ideological position that actively intervenes in the ideological confrontation represented by Fr. O'Connor and Mulhall. This is the ideology of Protestant liberalism and humanist concern, and if we include Yearling and the position he develops towards, and Fitz with the tendencies he expresses, the ideological map of Strumpet City now looks more complex.

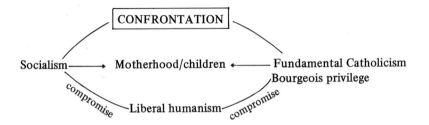

This suggests then, that *Strumpet City* is a search for an absent centre, the compromise between hostile and unbending ideologies. As such, we can now see how it links back to *A Week in the Life of Martin Cluxton* and *Tolka Row* and how, again, it reinforces the ideological project of Irish television over the last twenty years — the development of the liberal/social democratic discourse disguised by the nationalist consensus.

(iii) *Strumpet City* — Form and Conjuncture

I have, until now, concentrated on the mechanisms of characterisation in *Strumpet City*, in an attempt to demonstrate how deeper structures are at work and how these point to an ideological reading of the programme that a traditional literary concern with individual psychologies would disguise. However, I want to return now to the question of historical conjuncture, the ferment and change of Ireland in the 1980's, to show how *Strumpet City* avoids most of the strictures which McArthur locates in British television drama. By considering other aspects of formal organisation, as well as characterisation, I hope to show that *Strumpet City* also escapes the problems of *Tolka Row* with form and conjuncture.

McArthur's main argument in terms of British television history is that all the devices of narrative and the simplistic historiography they imply coalesce in producing a view of history which reconfirms dominant ideological assumptions in the Britain of the *present*. In concluding an analysis of two British series *Upstairs, Downstairs* and *Edward the Seventh* he summarises—

> However . . . they both represent superstructural activity in
> contemporary Britain, and as such, will show ideological similarities.
> The humanisation of the British Monarchy and the valorisation of
> Social Democracy constitute the best available terrain on which to
> fight for the maintenance of the socio-economic status quo.[27]

For McArthur, British historical drama serials speak not of the past in themselves, but of the present and support, indeed give cultural legitimacy to, the present British consensus operating around liberal welfarism, free-enterprise and the historical unity of the British state under the human face of its monarchy.

Strumpet City also addresses itself to the present, but the context in Ireland is very different. If, as I have been arguing, the ideological thrust of Irish television is towards supporting the *notion* of liberal welfarism, the fact remains that in Ireland in the '80's, there is no such fundamental consensus. Thus the ideological matrix in *Strumpet City* represented in the characters of Yearling, and, to a lesser extent, Fitz, has no contemporary reality to pin it down, or to anchor it chronologically in the present. In *Strumpet City,* these characters end in defeat — Yearling retiring from society bruised and beaten, Fitz going off to the trenches in France — and as ideological mouthpieces, they represent an absence, not just from history, but from the present. Thus the mothers and the children, Ireland herself, are all still presented as cast adrift in a hostile and uncaring vacuum. There is no final closure, as in the British context of the present consensus, but a continuation of struggle as in the Irish context of collapsing consensus.

I think that *Strumpet City* also gives clear indication of the nature of this present struggle and here, I think, it worth considering some key scenes in terms of structure and visual style. In visual terms, *Strumpet City* plays with the idea of constriction of space (represented by tight framing) and by the idea of escape. This is most clearly seen in the opening sequences of episode one but continues to be a recurrent motif throughout the seven episodes. And crucially, this motif has implications for the urban/rural discourse discussed earlier.

The opening shot is in one take, showing Mary's departure for life in the city from her country home. All the iconography of rural romanticism is present in this shot — the thatched cottage set among rolling green fields and framed by the hills in the background. As Mary stops, and waves goodbye to her family assembled around the cottage door, she is symbolically waving goodbye to the open space which this rural scene connotes and to the whole baggage of culturally specific meanings which the thatched cottage has accrued in Ireland.

As she walks away from the camera, moving down the hillside, Mrs. Bradshaw's voice-over is heard asking Mary if her father can read and write. The opening sequence of rural Ireland cuts at this point to the bourgeois opulence of the Bradshaw home showing Mary in attendance while Mrs. Bradshaw welcomes her to her new home. But this opulence is only a pause on Mary's eventual journey into further constriction. The rural naïveté of her statement "Please, Ma'am, I don't know where the kitchen is" is countered by Mrs. Bradshaw, "Why, downstairs of course". Mary's journey is well under way.

It is important to note some of the elements already introduced at this point. The city life which Mary will face is not that of the middle-class or indeed that of enlightenment, progress and culture which Raymond Williams sees at the heart of modern conceptions of the city (and perhaps highlighted by Mrs. Bradshaw's question concerning the reading and writing abilities of Mary's father). The city life which she will face is represented by Mr. Bradshaw's patriarchal authority — his restriction on sexuality ("Have the goodness to inform the young girl that company keeping will not be tolerated") and his defence of class privilege ("A spoiled servant is a bad servant").

After her short stay in the halfway environment of wealthy Kingstown, Mary's journey to further restriction of space in the inner city continues through her marriage to Fitz. The implications of this are set up visually in episode two.

Fitz proposes to Mary on the sand-banks of Dublin Bay, the same natural landscape used in the tramp sequences in *Martin Cluxton.* The camera holds them framed against the sky and the freedom of the location is underlined when Mary says that she wants to wait for a while. "Maybe it's because I'm from the country but I don't want to live in a house full of people." By waiting, she continues, they might be able to get a "little cottage" in the city.

A characteristic formal device of *Strumpet City* is juxtaposition between scenes, and in this sequence the dialectic between space and confinement is made clear. Mary and Fitz lie back on the sandbank as Mary says "Oh Fitz, look at the sky. Wouldn't it be terrible to be indoors on a day like this." The scene cuts immediately to a tight shot of Rashers in the prison cell. The policeman coming on duty declares ironically, "Not a bad evening".

The desire for escape is emphasised in nearly all the love scenes. Fitz and Mary, for example, first meet while both are escaping on the beach at Seapoint — he from the inner city, she from the stuffiness downstairs at the Bradshaws. The proposal scene, as we have seen, is on the sandbanks of Dublin Bay, and their decision to get married is taken in the natural surroundings of the Park.

Escape from the city is, of course, the central concern in the discourse about children. In terms of Mary's children, their escape was to be to Mary's family in the country although the workers' organisation plans to remove the children to the working-class homes of comrades in British cities.

The characteristic framing of *Strumpet City* is tight, medium close-ups or big close-ups, with minimal panning, tracking or high angle shots. In terms of an "epic", it is a remarkably constricted one. Perhaps an explanation for this is the fact that it was shot on location around Dublin and the destruction of the city over the last twenty years at the hands of property speculators limited the amount of camera movement. Just out of shot, one suspects, there is a glass office-block or a building-site crane. Whatever the reason, *Strumpet City,* in its visual style, reinforces the confinement that the characters feel.

The pivotal framing in *Strumpet City* is towards the end of episode seven. Rashers' rat-eaten corpse has been discovered in the basement and Fr. O'Connor rushes to help. He overcomes his disgust and nausea to take control of the situation. Making one final theological point ("It is not fitting that the brute beast should lie with the immortal soul") he has Rashers' dead dog removed. The camera holds the assembled company in a tight medium close-up, shot at a slight low angle from behind the corpse. Fr. O'Connor approaches, kneels down over Rashers, asks for forgiveness and proceeds with the prayers. The composition is crucial. In the tight confines of Rashers' basement, Fr. O'Connor is closest to the camera, shot from below, dominating the right hand half of the frame. In the background, to his left, Fitz kneels down, crosses himself and responds to the prayers. Slightly behind Fitz, Hennessy is seen, kneeling and praying also. Further back, the other residents are seen in solemn attention.

In the tight constricted world of *Strumpet City,* Fr. O'Connor, the mouthpiece of fundamental Catholicism, has assumed complete control and dominance. In formal terms, his victory is inscribed in the logic of both visual style and the dialectic of confinement and escape. There is no escape from Fr. O'Connor.

The framing of this slot affirms the victory of Fr. O'Connor and by extension, the rigid form of puritanical Catholicism which he represents. In historical terms then *Strumpet City* can be seen to analyse how the Church eventually overcame the oppositional forces of socialism and liberalism at a crucial moment in the formation of the modern Irish state. The victory that this represents does not, however, re-affirm a consensus, or a status quo, that exists in contemporary Ireland, as *Upstairs Downstairs* and *Edward The Seventh* does for constitutional monarchy and social democracy in contemporary Britain.

On the contrary, this victory is seen to be achieved at the expense of the more "natural" human feelings of the defeated and of great suffering for Ireland's children. The contemporary resonances are not re-affirmation of this victory, but a confirmation of the values of the defeated forces and an implicit acknowledgment that the struggle continues. Looked at in this light, the "closure" of the narrative is anything but complete, in the contemporary milieu. The reverse is more accurate.

Strumpet City attempts to open out hidden, disguised or temporarily defeated ideologies. It foregrounds the absence of a caring centre, of liberal social democracy, and at the same time opens out the possibility of other, more radical or more potentially subversive elements. The thrust of the narrative is towards social democracy, but the combination of its formal devices and the fissures in contemporary Ireland gives equal weighting to other oppositional elements. In conclusion I want to highlight some of these.

(a) Dialectical Struggle

Strumpet City operates in the main through a dialectical narrative movement. We have already seen how this worked in relation to the opposition of space and confinement in episode two, when the idyllic space of Dublin Bay is juxtaposed with the confinement of Rashers' prison cell. However, the serial operates this juxtaposition between scenes (and ideas) throughout, allowing the contrast between characters, their different milieux and their different philosophies to create its own dynamic of dialectical struggle. Thus in episode one, there is constant juxtaposition in the Bradshaws' between "upstairs" and "downstairs", linked by the differing attitudes of the characters to the Royal visit. There is contrast across class lines between the Bradshaws in Kingstown and the inner-city community in the slums and at times this contrast is used to highlight the huge disparities in wealth. For example, episode five opens with Rashers and Hennessy discussing (once again) where they would travel to if they had money (emphasising the recurring motif of escape). The scene ends with Rashers saying, "Well, if I was rich . . .". This sentence is cut short by the abrupt cut to a long shot of the interior of the opulent "Imperial Hotel" where Yearling and Fr. O'Connor are having dinner.

This juxtaposition between scenes is a constant device in *Strumpet City* and has the effect of foregrounding class division. The programme implicitly shows that the starkness of the worker's poverty is a prerequisite for the wealth of the ruling class. Indeed, if we consider the broad categories of characters again, divided as they are into class positions, we can see the fundamental reality of class relations clearly marked. If we invert the diagram into a triangular shape, we can see that the greater number of working class characters at the base are propping up the much smaller number of ruling class characters through the mediating support of the clergy.

Fr. O'Connor's victory, then, is a victory for the continuance of this mediating support and Bradshaw, the voice of bourgeois privilege, can retire from the scene, secure in the unbending support of Catholicism. What *Strumpet City* has to say about socialism is, therefore, crucial. A way of understanding this is provided by another use of juxtaposition, this time internal juxtaposition in a continuing sequence. This is best demonstrated in the scene described earlier, when Fitz helps Fr. O'Connor home from the workers' meeting.

The important element here is that Fitz is offering an arm to the distraught priest. Fitz leaves the meeting, literally walking away from his class allies to prop up the worried figure-head of Catholicism. As they leave the meeting behind, Fr. O'Connor recovers his composure long enough to warn Fitz about the dangerous men who have infiltrated the worker's movement with the evil doctrine of socialism. His remonstrations, indeed the very act of support and desertion by Fitz, are juxtaposed internally with the voice of the speaker who is heard declaring in the background that the bosses, the police and the clergy are the workers' enemies. The implication is clear.

The workers are acting against their best interests when they give support to their priests. Fitz's tendency to compromise, which is a positive virtue in a liberal sense is an act of treachery in the socialist sense. The defeat of Fitz and the absence of liberalism at the end is indictment enough of his compromising tendencies.

It is, therefore, a logic of the plot, that Fr. O'Connor's domination of the space left by Yearling's and Fitz's defeat can only be challenged by the equally intractable dogmatism of Mulhall and I think that the nature of Mulhall's removal from the plot is important.

Mulhall's death is presented as a slow withering decline resulting from the horrific industrial accident in which he loses both legs. His defeat can be seen as a symbolic castration of the ideological position he represents, that of militant socialism. But this defeat is not a result of any weakness of character, any innate flaw. It is a tragic working of fate, unlike Fitz's defeat, which is presented as largely self-inflicted. Mulhall's dogmatism is left unchallenged.

The final working out of the socialist view-point lends credence to the view that this struggle will continue and here, I think, the final denouement of the Pat Bannister/Lily Maxwell sub-plot is important.

Pat is presented throughout as Mulhall's closest deputy — in many instances he articulates more clearly the nature of the struggle. In episode five, for example, he declares — "Royalty will go, so will the exploiters". His commitment is as strong as Mulhall's (and Fr. O'Connor's) in terms of a tendency to violence, demonstrated clearly when he wrecks the pub as a ruse to distract police from protecting the scab workers. He echoes Mulhall's commitment by also going to prison for his violence and on his release again echoes Mulhall's comment that the prison regime failed to break his spirit.

In his relationship to Lily, Pat occupies a position more radically opposed to Fr. O'Connor's puritanism than even Mulhall does. Here the whole question of sexuality is broached in a clearer manner than anywhere else in the intricate structure of character and plot. Yearling only hints, in the most oblique and chaste manner possible, to his past sexual exploits. Fitz and Mary, the central sexual coupling, move through a conventional relationship that would receive Fr. O'Connor's warmest approval. Mulhall's relationship to his wife is affectionate, supportive, even touching in an emotional way. It is, however, remarkably restrained and untouching in a physical way, even when he returns home after six months in prison.

The only hints of active sexuality, oddly enough, are in relation to the two marginal workers, Hennessy and Lily. For Hennessy, it is a joke shared by himself and the others. Mulhall gruffly explains — "Jaysus, he only has to throw his trousers on the bed, and she's up the spout".

Hennessy echoes this when he says, to Mary's embarrassment, that the night watchman job will help to control the size of his family. But this is a conventional attitude to male sexuality — within marriage and resulting in pregnancy for the wife — again Fr. O'Connor would approve.

But in relation to Lily, the attitude is very different. She is a prostitute who uses her sexuality openly and for profit and despite the fact that this implies catering ultimately for the sexual needs of men, rather than for her own needs, the mere fact of her open sexuality is a rebuff to the repressed world of Fr. O'Connor and Bradshaw. Moreover, it is obvious that Lily and Pat are sexually active for their own pleasure, outside of marriage, and that Pat has scant respect for the decorum and institutions of marriage. For both, their relationship is geared to their own personal needs and not for the greater glory of God's design for procreation.

Viewed from the perspective of Fr. O'Connor, Pat and Lily are the most subversive couple in *Strumpet City* and the fact that the only real elements of hope and optimism are located in their relationship at the end adds weight to the feeling that from them will emanate the continuing struggle.

(b) *Strumpet City* **and Irish Nationalism**

I have described the consensus in Ireland up to the 1960s as one which operated around the concept of the historic Irish nation and that the appeal to this concept was mobilised around a notion of romantic rural community. It is therefore interesting to note the way in which *Strumpet City* negotiates the question of socialist struggle and nationalist struggle, given that the opposition between the city and the country invites an association of the city with class struggle and the country (the land) with the national struggle.

The context in contemporary Ireland of this dichotomy is an immensely complex one — indeed the breakdown of the nationalist consensus over the last two decades or so has had profound effects in Irish historiography, in the political party system, in the debates about a national culture, in attitudes to the continuing violence in Northern Ireland and in the crucial question of Church/State relationships.

The most frequent direct references to the national struggle are in episode one. Miss Gilchrist, for example, is given most of these direct references. She says to Mary as the Bradshaws prepare for the King's visit to Dublin —

> *"God be with the bold Fenian men . . . They were real men, not like them that's going nowadays."*

Later on she hopes that the cannon salute "will bring the rain peeing down on the lot of them."

However, if Miss Gilchrist, following the pattern of stereotyping leading to ideological position, is the mouthpiece for militant Fenianism, her fate within the plot is significant. First of all, she is childless and therefore there is no feeling within the plot that her Fenianism is being passed on. (This is of course, a judgment based on an analysis of *Strumpet City*'s aesthetics and not on an analysis of history.) By extension her death in the work-house, largely ignored and forgotten, underscores the fact that the ideology of militant nationalism which she espouses has nothing to offer in regard to the specific class struggles of the city.

The royal visit which annoys Miss Gilchrist so much, is on the other hand an opportunity to be used by the workers for their own ends. Fitz exploits it as an opportunity to meet Mary and for Rashers it is primarily an opportunity to make some money selling his "favours". Of course he is arrested for using the phrase "lousy Loyalists" but his anger is a result of being robbed of his money and not a statement of contempt for the King's presence, as is Miss Gilchrist's outburst.

In episode one, therefore, the nationalist discourse is raised and largely dismissed and does not permeate the workings of the narrative in the same way that the rural discourse does through the opposition of space and confinement.

Perhaps the place of nationalism in *Strumpet City*'s concern with working class struggles is best summarised by Pat Bannister. In episode five, Pat, Mulhall, Fitz and some others are in the pub, discussing the question of Sinn Féin. Pat is allowed the last comment when he says —

> *"Arthur Griffith and the Sinn Feiners – they're agin us, and Jim Larkin too".*

Pat and Lily represent the marriage of Socialism and the City — their optimism at the end, despite the seeming defeat around them, gives extra weight to Pat's comment on the national question.

Finally, the central concern of the narrative with the fate of the children implies a similar privileged position to a class-based, rather than a nationalist-based, solution. Mary wishes to send her children to her father in the country, a move approved by Fr. O'Connor. The combination here of rural and Catholic escape from the city is juxtaposed with a combination of urban and Protestant escape to England. Fr. O'Connor condemns the fact that Mary has given her money to Mrs Mulhall to provide a decent burial for her husband. He is, in fact, condemning Mary's good neighbourliness and class solidarity, raising the point that in her desperation Mary might consider sending her children to England.

The privileged position which the narrative gives to the confrontation at the dockside over the children implies just as clearly that the trans-national, class solidarity form of escape is approved over a rural escape, or Fr. O'Connor's desire to save souls. Again, therefore, *Strumpet City* rejects nationalist politics, mediated through the clergy, just as clearly as it rejects class oppression mediated through the clergy.

Conclusion

In terms of the cultural, political and ideological ferment in contemporary Ireland, *Strumpet City* is, I feel, a significant achievement. It provides a complex analysis of a key moment in the formation of the modern Irish State, foregrounding the class struggles of the urban working class and, perhaps more significantly, the role of the Church in containing Irish liberalism and Irish radicalism in favour of a conservative, Catholic state.

It speaks, therefore, to the present of the past. Its ideological thrust is towards a liberal social democratic consensus, in itself a profoundly radical break with dominant Church ideologies. However, through a combination of its own aesthetic devices and the ferment in contemporary Ireland, it opens up other, potentially more radical, modes of struggle. It is both a product of this contemporary ferment and addresses itself to it.

In terms of debates surrounding the ability of narrative forms to propose radical, or dialectical versions of the reality of struggle, it suggests, I think, that forms dictate contents only when the historical conjuncture offers a privileged mechanism for containing alternatives. The present conjuncture in Ireland offers no such mechanisms for final closure. Approached in this way, *Strumpet City* is a remarkably "open" text.

Finally, the extent of this achievement can provide a platform for discussing recent RTE co-productions — a way of gauging how the input of non-Irish factors — financial, cultural, institutional or ideological —possibly mediates the images and representation of Ireland so produced. This is another project.

REFERENCES

1. James Plunkett, *Strumpet City*, Hutchinson & Co. Ltd., 1969. Paperback — Panther Books, 1971.

2. For an account of the institutional importance of the serial for RTE, see John Kelleher, executive producer, 'What *Strumpet City* Means For RTE', in *Irish Broadcasting Review*, No. 8, Spring 1980.

3. For an account of the making of *The Year Of The French* and RTE's attitude to co-productions see Niall McCarthy, executive producer, 'The Year Of The French' in *Irish Broadcasting Review*, No. 14, Summer 1982.

4. Michael Collins, *The Path to Freedom*, Mercier Press, Cork 1968. Quoted in Maurice Goldring, *Faith of our Fathers*, Repsol Publishing, Dublin 1982.

5. See Joseph Lee, (ed.), *The Age of De Valera*, Ward River Press, Dublin 1982.

6. Joseph Lee, 'Society and Culture" in Frank Litton (ed.), *Unequal Achievement*, Institute of Public Administration, Dublin 1982.

7. For a full discussion of the relationship between literature, ideology and society see Terry Eagleton, *Criticism And Ideology*, New Left Books 1976, especially chapter 4 —'Ideology and Literary Form'.

8. Eagleton, *op. cit.*

9. For a full discussion of the Heaven/Hell antinomy see Raymond Williams 'The Welsh Industrial Novel' in *Problems In Materialism And Culture*, Verso Editions and New Left Books, London 1980.

10. Eagleton, *op. cit.*

11. Bishop MacNamee of Ardagh and Clonmacnoise, *The Cinema*, Feb. 10th, 1937. Quoted in Kevin Rockett, *Film And Ireland: A Chronicle*, A Sense of Ireland Ltd. 1980. Available from the Irish Film Institute.

12. Raymond Williams, *The Country And The City*, Chatto and Windus 1973. Paperback, Paladin 1975.

13. For a full discussion of nineteenth century English literature and its image of country and city, see Raymond Williams, *The Country And The City*, especially chapters 17 to 22 incl.

14. *Tolka Row*, episode 36, tx 3/6/68. Written by Colin Bird, produced by Brian Mac Lochlainn. There is no national film and television archive in Ireland. RTE developed a policy for preserving broadcast material only in the early 1970s, so a lot of 1960s material is unfortunately lost.

15. Wesley Burrowes, *The Riordans*, Gilbert Dalton, Dublin 1977. Page 6.

16. See Kevin Rockett, 'Film Censorship and the State' in *Film Directions*, Vol. 3, No. 9, Jan. 1980.

17. For a discussion of the documentary drive in British television drama see '*Television Documentary/Drama*', BFI Dossier 19, British Film Institute 1982.

18. Colin McArthur, 'Television and History', *BFI Television Monograph* 8, British Film Institute 1978.

19. For a full discussion of the constrictions of narrative, see Colin MacCabe, 'Realism And The Cinema: Notes On Some Brechtian Theses' in *Screen*, Vol. 15, No. 2, Summer 1974. MacCabe defines traditional narrative as "classic realist texts". Such narratives, he continues cannot deal with the "real" in its contradictions and that they offer the reader (or viewer) a fixed point of view from which everything becomes obvious.

20. See, for example, *Dublin 1913 – A Divided City*, produced for second level school students by the Curriculum Development Unit and published by O'Brien Press 1978. This short text book covers the same period as *Strumpet City*, placing the events in the wider contexts of world politics and introducing economic, social and class factors.

21. See Robert Kee, *The Green Flag*, Weidenfeld & Nicholson, London 1972.

22. McArthur, *op. cit.*, chapter 10.

23. See Colin McArthur, 'Days of Hope" in *Screen*, Vol. 16, No. 4, Winter 1975/76. In this article, McArthur posits the idea of a "progressive realist text" in opposition to MacCabe's "classic realist text" and argues that within classic narrative structures a sense

of the real as contradictory can be achieved through juxtaposition. Neither writer mentions historical conjuncture, which is, I feel, the final determining factor in how "open" or "closed" realist texts will be read.

24. See Richard Dyer, *Stars,* British Film Institute 1979.

25. Terence de Vere White, *Irish Times,* reproduced in *Strumpet City,* Panther edition 1971.

26. The original letter from the Archbishop of Dublin, William D. Walsh, is quoted in full in *Dublin 1913, op. cit.* The reality is as illuminating as its fictional mouthpiece, Fr. O'Connor.

27. McArthur, 'Television And History', *op. cit.*

4   Twenty Years of Current Affairs on RTE

Mary Kelly

Because current affairs programming has come to play an accepted and central role as a major source of information, comment and communication about Irish society, it is often forgotten how recent its origin is. The development of current affairs on television, as we know it, did not really take off until the late 1960s. It should be remembered in particular that there was no political comment or discussion of controversial subjects on Radio Éireann until the 1950s. During this latter decade, however, some small steps forward were taken: party political broadcasts were initiated for the 1954 general election and the proceedings in the Dáil and Senate were summarised in a weekly programme entitled *'The Week in Leinster House'*. Maurice Gorham in his history of the first forty years of Radio Éireann recounts, "The new feature met with general approval in the Dáil; almost the only criticism came from one Deputy who said Inglis (the presenter) flattered the speakers — he made them sound more intelligent than they really were."[1]

Until the mid 1960s, politicians, frequently under instruction from political parties, were often loath to take part in discussion programmes either on radio or on television. Jack White, the first head of current affairs on the newly initiated Telefís Éireann, noted in 1962 that while he hoped "to see many of our politicians before the cameras in the next twelve months," he recognised that some "politicians find the prospect rather alarming."[2] Before 1966 politicians appeared only occasionally on such magazine programmes as *'Broadsheet'* and on the outside broadcast programme *'Open House'* which had a politicians' panel to answer questions from members of local communities.

In 1966 the programme *'Division'* began with reporters Paddy Gallagher, Ted Nealon and David Thornley. Its brief was to explicitly concern itself with Irish politics, through interviews and discussions.

RTE named the party member it wanted to appear and this invitation was passed through the party whip to the politician in question. The interviews were frequently rather gentlemanly affairs, low key and leisurely, with the interviewer seeking information and discursive elaboration on a particular topic rather than undertaking aggressive or 'hard' questioning on controversial issues. For example, Charles Haughey, in 1966 Minister for Finance, was interviewed by Paddy Gallagher about the upcoming budget. They discussed how, in general, budgets come to be formulated, the role of the civil service and cabinet, its social and economic functions, the consequences of direct and indirect taxation, and whether Haughey, as an accountant, was especially well qualified to formulate a budget. Haughey, apparently well aware of a too obvious lack of humility on television, kicked this last question gracefully to touch — while at the same time leaving no illusions as to his competence and qualifications. Even at this stage, Haughey had a smooth TV image — not too cocky or aggressive, informative, direct, 'straight'. Occasionally, however, some mildly controversial material did surface — as when the General Secretary of Fine Gael described contributors to Fianna Fáil's party fund (TACA) as "buying favours".

During the early and mid-sixties period the RTE Authority stood firm on the relative independence it had been granted by the state in the Broadcasting Act of 1960. This independence was dependent on the Authority fulfilling a series of conditions, one of which was ensuring that "When it broadcasts any information, news or feature which relates to matters of public controversy or is the subject of current public debate, the information, news or feature is presented objectively and impartially and without any expression of the Authority's own views."[3]. The Authority interpreted this as requiring fairness and 'balance' in programmes. Balance was to be secured by giving the different sides of a story, or by having the representatives of the contentious or conflicting views on the programme and ensuring that the chairperson gave them adequate time in which to present their case.

Despite the low key nature of reporting and discussion and the strict norms of balance, RTE came under criticism from politicians, especially the Taoiseach Seán Lemass, for its treatment of governmental affairs on news and current affairs, culminating in his well known Dáil statement in 1966 that RTE:

> was set up by legislation as an instrument of public policy and as such was responsible to the Government. The Government had overall responsibility for its conduct and especially the obligation to ensure that its programmes do not offend against the public interest, or conflict with national policy as defined in legislation. To this extent the Government reject the view that RTE should be, either generally or in regard to its current affairs programmes and news programmes, completely independent of Government supervision.[4]

Todd Andrews who was appointed Chairman of the RTE Authority at the same time notes in his recent autobiography that he was "fully in agreement" with Lemass on this score:

> *This point of view was even more strongly held by me because I had had very definite and sometimes sorry experiences of the consequences of resistance to government policies by some of the semi-state bodies and even by civil servants.*[5]

Lemass's statement as to the limits of RTE's autonomy and the ultimate authority of the government to ensure that programmes did not "offend against the public interest or conflict with national policy" was made precisely at the time when current affairs programming was beginning to take-off In RTE, especially the programme *'7 Days'*. It did not halt these developments: relative to the leisurely and gentlemanly discussions of previous years, new current affairs programmes had a greater tendency to raise controversial political and social topics, and to question politicians and other elites more directly. Nonetheless, the shape of these programmes, their style of presentation and their treatment of topics were undoubtedly influenced to some degree by the delicate institutional position of RTE relative to the state. This of course is not at all peculiar to RTE, all public service television stations in European countries are closely influenced by their relationship to the state and to the society of which they are a part.[6]

Below I shall examine two pervasive elements in current affairs programming styles, both of which have been centrally influenced by the socio-political system within which RTE operates. These are, firstly, the extent to which current affairs programmes have established a 'personality system' of well-known presenters whose very familiarity, status and style lends authority and credibility to the programme, and thus contributes to its ability to raise controversial issues regarding those in power; and, secondly, the extent to which current affairs programmes have attempted to articulate a 'middle ground' ideologically speaking, a middle position which is both sufficiently tolerable to significant elites and readily intelligible to a sufficiently large section of the viewers.

The Personality System

In 1967 *'Division'* was amalgamated with *'7 Days'* which had also begun the previous year. This brought two teams of experienced reporters together: John O'Donoghue, Brian Cleeve and Brian Farrell from *'7 Days'* and Paddy Gallagher, Ted Nealon and David Thornley from the old *'Division'* programme. It was broadcast twice weekly, and many of the main characteristics of current affairs programming as we know them became established at this point — as well as current affairs programmes becoming very popular with the audience.

One of the central characteristics of the *'7 Days'* programme was its establishment of a 'personality system'. In current affairs this means having a team of trusted and credible presenters who appear, week in and week out, fronting the programme, giving it a sense of televisual identity and an authoritative style. Establishing a viable 'personality system' is important to the programme makers, to the station as a whole, and to the viewers.[7]

In a current affairs programme which aims to cover controversial subjects and to be up-to-date, it is essential to be able to change plans quickly, to take decisions at the last minute and to go out live. Such a programme requires a 'frontman', a presenter or interviewer who can be trusted, even under strain, not to collapse. As Lelia Doolan, an early producer of '7 Days' noted of its presenters, not only were they "already well known to the public, and trusted by them,"[8] but "they could always be depended upon to give the programme an air of thoughtful deliberation and authority"[9] whatever the mayhem behind the scenes.

Equally important is to have a group of presenters who can be trusted by the broadcasting organisation to exercise 'due care' and 'sensitivity' in relation to the socio-political system in which broadcasting works. As we have seen, the government and the Dáil have powers over broadcasting, and may, if they wish, have the last say — a power which they have not been slow to use in banning interviews with members of proscribed organisations since the mid 1970's. It is thus in the interests of broadcasting organisations such as RTE to exercise 'due care' in order to hold onto what independence they have. Many media researchers in Britain have noted similar interests and consequent behaviour in the case of the BBC. One way of attempting to ensure 'due care' is exercised is by having a small number of well trusted presenters. An ex-current affairs producer of the BBC has noted:

> it is through the recruitment and deployment of a remarkably small body of professional communicators that the BBC has sought to walk the tightrope that it has to between the drop on one side into utter governmental dependence, and on the other into suicidal opposition to it.[10]

He notes of these presenters that:

> "Their professional skills, their cultivation of a particular style, their public standing and reputation establish for the BBC a necessary, even though limited insulation from its environment. On the one hand they can hold their own with politicians and other public figures. They hold off the absorption of the BBC by the state. On the other hand they are strategically deployed in the system of control of both contributors and producers. In this way, they prevent potentially dangerous embarrassment to the organisation, by inhibiting the expression of attitudes that openly flout the codes, political and moral, of the powers-that-be.[11]

I would argue that this also holds true of the central group of presenters of current affairs programmes on RTE, at present including Brian

Farrell, John Bowman, Pat Kenny, John O'Donoghue and Olivia O'Leary.

There are two modes whereby presenters may come to establish the credibility of their pronouncements in the public eye. One is by taking an authoritative stance which may also be somewhat aggressive, sceptical and aloof. However, despite aggressive questioning, forms of polite address will be constantly adhered to: "With respect, Minister . . .", "Can we now move onto . . ." etc. 'Authoritative' presenters may often bring accreditation to this stance by their position in other status-giving occupations, especially in the university (Farrell, Thornley) or in newspapers or radio (Bowman, O'Leary). They also seek further accreditation by aligning themselves with the authority of 'the expert' and the professionals on the programme — when, that is, they are not setting themselves up as the expert against all-comers.

A second mode of establishing credibility is for presenters to identify themselves with 'you, the viewers', to be populist and common-sensical and thus forge an identification with the audience. Such interviewers seek "to be accepted by the audience as their representative, speaking for them."[12] In this mode of address the use of personal pronouns is extremely important — it is 'You' the viewers, and 'We' both the viewers and presenters together, and 'Them' i.e. those who behave contrary to accepted values. This mode of address can be exemplified in the way John O'Donoghue introduced the '7 Days' programme on illegal money-lending, transmitted in November 1969:

> *Good evening, How much do you owe on your house, your car, your fridge? Do you owe back income tax? Have you an overdraft in the bank and not enough money to pay your bills? You're not unusual, if that is your situation. In this country, collectively, we owe nearly £700 million which works out at about £250 per head of population. The worst that happens most of us if we can't pay our bills is that we reduce our standard of living or borrow from more or less sympathetic sources. But there are those whose bills are for the very necessities of life and if they can't pay, they're often afraid of their lives. These are the people who fall into the hands of unlicensed money-lenders.*
>
> *(This statement was followed by a 'teaser' – a dramatic statement by an unlicensed money-lender which not only tempted the audience to stay with the programme but vouched for the 'reality' and credibility of the presenter's claims:*
> *Unlicensed money-lender:)*
>
> *Well, I say to them: 'I want your man broken up well – I don't care how bad, once you don't kill him. Let it be his arm or legs – give him a good doing'.*
> *(O'Donoghue again:)*
>
> *It sounds melodramatic. You may say it couldn't happen, but it does.*
> *(Journalist on the film . . .)*

The populist mode may also be integrated with the more authoritative mode. An example of this was the interviewing of Kevin Boland, then Minister for Local Government, by David Thornley. The issue on hand was the dismissal of Dublin Corporation by Boland in 1969, when the Corporation refused to strike a higher rate, on the grounds that health · services should not be financed from local rates but from taxation. Thornley was enabled to ask hard hitting questions by aligning himself with "the ordinary voters and citizens of Dublin" and with "responsible local democracy" as represented by Dublin Corporation. He could thus make statements like, "The ordinary citizens of Dublin . . . voted for the ex-corporation members," and "The members of Dublin Corporation have examined (the financing of health charges from taxation rather than rates) and come to the conclusion that the financing of health services from taxation is a fairer way. And, with respect, who are you to say that that is an opinion they are not entitled to hold?" Boland, in a very typical political response, aligned himself, not of course with anti-democratic forces, but with the superior wisdom of the "national interest", replying, "Politicians must be willing to do the unpopular thing in the national interest."

Given that current affairs presenters are on the one hand questioning those with power and that on the other they must attempt to communicate effectively with their audience, they need an intelligible and · acceptable middle ground from which to question and probe. They need to align themselves with the opinions of other high status groups (e.g. 'experts' and professionals), with 'the people', or with some other central political or cultural value to which there is a relatively high degree of common consent (e.g. a general belief in responsible democracy and the need for honest government).

Having aligned themselves with this middle ground, presenters have many advantages in establishing it as the most correct, appropriate, natural and 'balanced' stance. Current affairs programmes are frequently transmitted twice weekly and can run to as much as four nights a week — as has recently been the case with *Today Tonight'*. The style and format of the programmes tend to be highly ritualised and repetitive: the same studio set, the same group of presenters, the same limited set of programme formats (a mix of studio discussion and filmed reports being the most usual), the same authoritative military style music introducing the programme emphasising its immediacy and urgency. In this ritualised performance the presenter is a crucial aspect of the programme's televisual identity.[13] She/he is essential in creating regularity, predictability and familiarity. The camera cuts to the presenter: she/he presents the programme menu, frequently framing it authoritatively in terms of such news-values as immediacy, elite involvement and elite conflict, and drawing on 'expert' sources to legitimate and importance of the topic. An examination of the introductory sequence of a *'Today Tonight'* programme transmitted in

December 1981, and in which there were two items — a studio discussion with the Minister for the Gaeltacht and a filmed report on the mainly working class housing area of Finglas — exemplifies these processes.

The programme opened with a close-up of the Minister for the Gaeltacht, with Brian Farrell's voice, authoritative and staccato, outlining the programme menu: "The Minister of the Gaeltacht on the government's decision to cry halt on Knock Airport, and . . .", the camera cut to a close-up of two published reports, ". . . Finglas, a case study of deprivation." The visuals vouched for the 'reality', authority and expertness of the presenter's words and for the subsequent programme. The introductory sequence continued with a long shot of the darkened *'Today Tonight'* studio, with the Minister and Brian Farrell seated in the distance, facing each other across their desks. The beat of the *'Today Tonight'* music came up, dramatic and staccato, while to its beat, the programme title: TODAY TONIGHT was printed up brightly and predominantly. The studio lighting came up, the camera cut immediately to a close-up of Brian Farrell stating directly to the camera:

> *Later in the programme we present one side of a divided city: the case from Finglas. But first that terse announcement this evening by the government that the much publicised and controversial Knock Airport is to be cut off. And the man at the centre of what is bound to be a major political and regional storm, (camera cuts to the Minister) Paddy O'Toole, Minister for the Gaeltacht, and Fine Gael Deputy for East Mayo. (The camera cuts back to Brian Farrell turning to the Minister) Minister, you talk about postponing, deferring, you really mean abandoning don't you?*

He thus drew on the news-values of immediacy, elite involvement, controversy and conflict, establishing the importance of the item and his own central role in investigating it, while his authority to ask 'hard questions' was authenticated by the established nature and credibility of the programme, ritually maintained and reproduced in the programme music and logo, by the close-ups of the presenter — familiar week in and week out to the viewers, and by his own terse style. As has been noted of TV's 'personality system' in current affairs: "events change, (but) the TV personality, the focus of the programme identity, carries on. The real world may be unstable and unbalanced, but the world of the TV presenters who explain that world to us is not."[14] And again, "The very repetition of their appearances week after week, supports the authority of their wisdom. The way they make sense of the world becomes more authoritative, paternalistic."[15]

Presenters, TV journalists and producers have the power, consistently each week to frame the discussion in a particular way, to establish, as Stuart Hall suggests, a preferred reading of the topic by employing "particular codes and their combination . . . so as to produce and sustain, not *the* meaning (for there is no such unitary thing) but the *preferred encoding* of the topic."[16] The use of visual encoding to produce a preferred reading of a topic can be exemplified by analysing some aspects of the *'Today Tonight'* programme entitled 'The Roscommon File', transmitted in December 1982. This filmed report was concerned with the then Minister for Justice, Seán Doherty, and his alleged interference with the Gardaí in his own Roscommon constituency. It is perhaps a particularly interesting example of the way in which the authoritativeness and credibility of the programme and its presenters were established both verbally and visually in such a potentially sensitive area.

The programme began with a teaser: a clip from the filmed report, showing close-ups of first, Derek Nally, General Secretary of the Association of Garda Sergeants and Inspectors, and then of the local parish priest, Canon Dodd, suggesting (or more correctly, being gently prodded by the reporter into suggesting) that the Minister for Justice was engaged in political interference in Gardaí affairs. The credibility of the programme was thus straight away vouched for by such respectable and authoritative opinion as that of the local Canon. Indeed it is possible that the programme might not have gone ahead in such a tough uncompromising form, if the Canon had not in fact lent his weight to it. Clips from Canon Dodd's interview were used throughout the programme to the same effect, as were similar allegations from the local G.P. and the editor of the local newspaper.

The introductory teaser continued with a low angled shot of the Minister for Justice on an election platform in Roscommon, followed by a picture of the local Garda Sergeant, Tully, walking alone in a wood. In voice over, the anchorman, John Bowman, introduced the programme as "An investigation of allegations of political interference with the Gardaí in Roscommon", followed by the beat of the *'Today Tonight'* music and logo. Cutting to the studio, John Bowman, now in close-up, sketched in briefly, in a level, authoritative tone, directly to camera, the wider political and national context of this report: the fact that the issue of an independent police authority which would "guarantee the Gardaí freedom from political interference" had been "flirted with" by various governments over the past ten years but nothing further had been done. He also made a gesture to political 'balance' in stating:

> *But political interference is a charge as old as politics and many ministers have been accused of it. Where the Gardaí are concerned little has ever been proved. Allegations of political interference, for example, have been made against former coalition Minister, Jim Mitchell, as well as against previous Ministers for Justice. Tonight we look at the relations between the Guards and their present Minister who is a native of Roscommon, a TD for Roscommon and himself a former member of the Gardaí Síochána.*

Moving on to the filmed report, the reporter, Pat Cox immediately established the main story line: "Central to what we will call The Roscommon File has been a battle of wills between the Minister, Mr. Doherty and the local Sergeant, Tom Tully. On the one hand a Cabinet

Minister determined to show his power in his own backyard, on the other an iron-willed Sergeant determined to apply the Rule of Law rigorously and equally between all citizens." This statement was accompanied by a close up of a 'file' to which was attached a photo of the two main protagonists. Throughout the film these two protagonists were represented visually quite differently: O'Doherty was represented as something of a demagogue at an election meeting, surrounded by ya-hooing supporters, or in his official·capacity reviewing passing-out parades of Gardaí at Tullamore, or by shots of the Department of Justice in Dublin. Tully on the contrary was represented as walking alone or being alone even in a crowd. He was the loner, upstanding protector of the law. Cinematic imagery and symbolism of the 'lone hero' wasn't far off. Indeed dramatised visual imagery was consistently used to carry the journalist's story: the ringing phone and a hand crossing to pick it up; a car swerving; the introduction of each new case against O'Doherty with a file carrying his photo, 'The Roscommon File' stamped in large red letters across it, and the title of each 'case' of interference labelling it.

To summarise. When a 'personality system' is well established within current affairs programming, the authority of the presenters tends to be visually and verbally confirmed by weekly appearances, by the ritual of the televisual style of the programme, by the familiarity of its sets and formats, by its logo and music, by the predictability of the presenters' styles. These styles may range from the highly authoritative, sceptical and abrasive through to the populist — being one with 'you' the viewers, asking questions on 'your' behalf, standing with 'the people' and 'democracy' against the activities of certain elites and bureaucracies. The establishment of such a 'personality system' of tried and tested presenters not only contributes to the televisual identity of the programme (and indeed of a TV station as a whole), and to the persuasiveness with which the presenters can put forward their preferred reading of the topic under discussion, but lends the programme sufficient authority to raise controversial issues and to ask contentious questions — within certain limits of course. However, such a well established personality system as exists at present on *'Today Tonight'* also tends to allow the occasional breaching of these limits, and thus the redefining of new boundaries as to what are considered appropriate issues to raise and questions to ask. Thus the areas of allowable investigative reporting may be slowly broadened, although undoubtedly, 'due care' and sensitivity to the socio-political system within which broadcasting organisations operate also need to be constantly maintained.

Articulating a Middle Ground

As noted above, current affairs presenters need to articulate a 'middle ground' which will incorporate both a sufficiently acceptable launching pad from which they can question and probe those with power and status, and a range of values which can be relatively easily understood by the audience. Views which could be seen as too extreme might readily lead to the easy dismissal of presenters by both interviewees and the audience as 'unrealistic' and 'unreasonable'. The middle ground which they articulate must be seen as 'reasonable' and pragmatic. It must either be aligned with the views of a sufficiently large and relevant elite or combination of elites, and/or express those values about which there is sufficient consensus within the society.

In RTE, current affairs personnel have generally aligned themselves with a middle ground which is progressive and social democratic. They have aligned themselves with:

—parliamentary democracy and its forms of debate and discussion
—dutiful, responsive, honest and efficient government
—'public opinion' and 'the people' — as interpreted by the presenters themselves
—the opinion of the expert, the professional and high status journalists
—a belief in the possibility of ameliorating social problems, conflict and injustice by piecemeal reform and progressive improvements usually to be undertaken by the state.

They have aligned themselves against:

—official neglect, inefficient or unfeeling officialdom
—dishonest and inefficient government
—the lack of state policies, social services and institutions to deal with social problems and social conflict
—speculators and profiteers
—individuals who promote violence, crime, drugpushers etc.

The values articulated in current affairs programmes have been predominantly of the 'Just Society'[17] variety, liberal and progressive with a sufficient tinge of moral indignation to criticise existing entrenched elites, bureaucracies and what are seen a non-progressive conservative forces. Overwhelmingly those given time to express and elaborate these views, whether as presenters or interviewees, have been male and middle class.[18] Below I will outline some aspects of the middle ground as articulated in political discussions, in the presentation of trade union activities, and in relation to the coverage of social problems.

The typical format for political discussions on current affairs has been that of the presenter either quizzing an individual party or parliamentary representative, or chairing a discussion between such representatives. In both cases it is the presenter who introduces, frames and orchestrates interventions from the politicians concerned, calls forth responses, stimulates conflict and yet also contains it within the norms of what are considered acceptable and rational means of expressing disagreement. The participating politicians have rights to upstage each other in argument (but not to hog the microphone), indeed outwitting the opponent is seen as the point of the exercise, but strictly within the rules of awaiting one's turn as signalled and policed by the presenter. The presenter initiates and interposes questions, often in the name of 'the people': "What the people want to know is . . .?" or in the name of 'expert opinion': "But what the . . . report makes clear is . . ., what is the government going to do about that?" or in the name of the opposition: "But won't the opposition be right in claiming . . .?"

This form of discussion and argument is based on and symbolically reproduces many of the accepted norms and values of parliamentary democracy: the belief in 'rational' public discussion between opponents, the right of the opposition to publicly question government policies, the requirement that politicians be able to defend their policies when challenged, the right of 'experts' and 'the people' to question government policy and action. However the television format interposes of course a third party — the presenter — into the scene, a party with perhaps an unequalled power to frame the discussion in a particular manner, to draw on his/her interpretation of 'public opinion', of 'the national interest', of the opinion of the opposition, of 'the state of the nation', 'the extent of the recession' and to call up expert witnesses as suits. This power may be somewhat disguised by the 'chairperson' role — the 'neutral' arbiter — which the presenter plays. Yet the chairperson role does have its limits: she/he must not be seen as too obviously biased or unfair, but rather as detached and non-partisan between sectional interests. The presenter is thus constrained to stay within the limits of what are considered fair and balanced questions, what is considered 'common sense'. The pull is thus constantly towards 'reasonable' questions, drawing on the middle ground of sufficient consensus and common sense.

In current affairs coverage of industrial relations and trade union activity the format again tends to be that of discussions between contending interests, in which the discussion symbolically represents the existing and accepted relationships between union, employer and, where appropriate, government. During the 1960s and 70s, the unions and especially the ICTU were to a degree incorporated into the Irish state. There were seen as responsible institutions whose cooperation was needed to expedite industrial and national development.[19] The unions have been seen, especially perhaps by Fianna Fáil governments,[20] as one of the 'social partners' who have an essential role to play in planning and accomplishing industrial development, in membership of many state appointed advisory boards and in formulating national pay policy.

Current affairs programmes have in many instances reproduced in the format and style of its programmes on industrial relations this structure of power relationships. However, conflict between contending parties is often seen as making 'good television' and as holding audience interest, and thus in, for example, a strike situation or in a situation where there are political rumblings regarding the need to curb union power, the presenter may attempt by the kinds of questions asked to set up a confrontation situation. In general, union representatives on such programmes have been able to query unpalatable definitions of union activity, have been given sufficient time to do so, as well as time to suggest a broader role for the unions than one to one employer-union conflict. An early example of this was on a 1964 programme entitled 'Trade Unionism in Ireland' presented by John O'Donoghue. After briefly sketching in the historical development of trade unions in Ireland, he continued:

> *One of the central questions about trade unions is what to do about a militant union which, by going on strike without full consultation with other unions, puts them out of work. Workers themselves and the community are damaged by irresponsible action on the part of the union and the question has to be raised that there should be machinery to force a union to act responsibly.*

He elaborated on this in terms of the suggestion that the government bring in legislation which would institute legal controls over such 'irresponsible' activity, or whether the trade unions themselves should or could "impose discipline on unions who are not acting responsibly" — either towards other workers or the community. In reply, Barry Desmond, then Industrial Officer of the ICTU, stated:

> *What exactly do we mean by this term 'irresponsibility'? You use these terms 'control', 'irresponsibility' 'sanctions by the unions'. I think the most disgraceful part of this attitude on the part of some politicians in particular is that they completely misunderstand the function and structure of the trade union movement.*

He continued by stating that the trade unions could manage their own internal affairs, especially through the sanctions of the ICTU,[21] while later in the programme he argued that it was in the trade union movement's own interest to become more closely involved in the political management of the economy:

> *... the standard of living of workers, wages, budgets form the political aspects of the economy and thus the unions of this country have a direct influence on the political and social structure of our economy. Unions if they want to consolidate, if they want political influence to effect standards of living, will have to have a big political say in this country.*

The dynamics influencing the coverage of 'social problem' groups — i.e. groups who frequently lack power, privilege and status — are quite different from those influencing the coverage of the powerful, including politicians, industrialists and trade unions. In the latter the typical form of coverage, as noted above, is the studio discussion in which members of these elite groups represent their own interests, firmly organised and orchestrated by the chairperson in terms of 'balanced' turn-taking by the different sides. In the coverage of 'social problem' groups — usually

100

through filmed reports — 'experts', professionals and media personnel tend to speak 'for' the group in question, along with a tiny minority from the group itself. This minority tends to be chosen not by the members of the group but by media personnel, frequently on the basis of their ability to articulate in televisual terms the storyline of the programme. The representativeness — or more precisely the lack of representativeness — of this minority has caused criticism of current affairs coverage of some working class communities such as Finglas and Ballyfermot.

In the programme on Finglas (*'Today Tonight'*, December 1981), the presenter's storyline of "the reality of multiple deprivation" leading to "potential social breakdown" was 'confirmed' not only by the presenter's words, backed up by professional and ministerial authority, but by the statements of a handful of local residents, and in particular, perhaps, the close-ups of their tense and worried faces. At the end of the programme the presenter was able to claim, "The people in Finglas, they talk of a crunch on the way, a cancer spreading, an explosion, that's their picture." However, as subsequent criticism of the programme from within Finglas itself was to show, the representativeness of the locals on the programme was very much open to question — inevitably perhaps — given the handful of residents on the programme about a community of some 50,000, the size of Galway.

Often in coverage of working class areas current affairs personnel appear to have been insensitive to the range of differences in status, wealth and 'respectability' within working class communities. Sociological studies have consistently highlighted the variability from 'roughs' through to 'respectables', and the dynamics of the interrelationship between these groups which characterise such communities. Yet current affairs reporting frequently represent working class housing estates as homogeneous — and as constituting a major social problem.

One example of this was the coverage of Ballyfermot by a *'7 Days'* report in 1971. This report characterised the estate as "a veritable concrete jungle", on an apparent "downward spiral", in which problems "are a vicious cycle beginning with the children, if they don't get a square deal everything goes wrong and the cycle starts all over again, because many in Ballyfermot marry their own often crowding in with in-laws." As for the children: "what about the one-third who don't make the grade — who are either educationally subnormal or emotionally disturbed?" The presenter characterised the community as having "few facilities, and boys who hang around inevitably get into trouble. The problems of truancy and boredom are dumped into the laps of the Gardaí (shots of two Gardaí patrolling with an alsatian dog), with the resultant antagonism between the young people and the forces of law and order." These views were 'confirmed' by interviews with doctors and teachers.

However, Ballyfermot Community Association did not like this characterisation of their community. Not only was there a discussion programme on the film the following week, but later there was another filmed report regarding Ballyfermot in which members of the Community Association played a central role. This described the development of neighbourhood units in Ballyfermot, the development of local interest groups, the local newspaper and local democracy, ending with, "Ballyfermot is definitely on the way." Seeing the two films, one could hardly guess that the same community was being represented!

The problem of labelling groups as a 'social problem' is not of course a media creation. The media represents and confirms an existing structure of power in our society which gives the right and power to certain elites — especially perhaps professionals and those concerned with the maintenance of law and order — to publicly label other groups, especially those groups who are weaker and more disadvantaged.

Current affairs programmes, especially filmed reports, often attempt to create and sustain the illusion that the film they create represents *the reality*. They attempt to state 'This is Finglas', 'This is Darndale', 'This is the drug problem in Dublin today'. A film is of course a highly selective symbolic representation of some aspects of a situation, selected and formulated into a televisual story which will, it is hoped, hold the audience's attention. Current affairs attempts to carry the journalistic myth that reality can be represented in an unmediated way, by holding up a mirror. The burden of proof that 'this is reality' lies not only in the opinions of experts, the authority of the presenter or verbal statements by members of the problem group, it lies — and often very significantly so — in the visual representation: the camera panning along the row upon row of corporation houses, the derelict sites, the rubbish. In the *'Today Tonight'* programme on the Corporation estate of Darndale (May 1983), the presenter, having outlined the planners' dream for the community, stated, "That was the dream, the reality is quite different", as she stands in front of a scruffy and badly kept playground: 'the reality' is proved.

In programmes on social problems the typical format is to give over most of the programme to confirming the existence of the problem — through authenticating visuals, the words of select community members and the authoritative accreditation of experts and the presenter — and at the very end to propose some form of social democratic solution: massive state investment is needed, a job creation programme, higher investment in education, improvement in housing and the environment, official lethargy or mal-administration must be overcome. How these changes may be brought about or financed are rarely discussed, and there is little deeper analysis of the causes of the social problem. Indeed if the programmes were to attempt to analyse the social structural foundations of many social problems and the difficulties posed in eradicating them, the programme might well be accused of reaching beyond the common consensus which is concerned with so-called 'realism', and pragmatism, what is happening in the here and now, not with analysing or abolishing the conditions from which the problem arises in the first place.

Discussion

Two major constraints have influenced the development of current affairs' televisual codes over the past 20 years. The first is the need for 'due care' in the face of powerful elite groups, while the second is the need to capture and hold audience interest. The argument of this chapter has been that these constraints have contributed both to the establishment of a personality system of well-known, authoritative and professional presenters, and to the need for these presenters to elaborate a readily intelligible and consensus oriented middle ground, although conflict within the bounds of this consensus is highlighted and indeed encouraged often in the interest of its presumed attractiveness to the audience.

Current affairs programming is a potentially dangerous arena for any broadcasting organisation. Programmes on the activities of political and other powerful elites, on conflicts between them, on ineptitudes and inefficiencies may easily fan the flames of a desire to contain and limit the independence of the broadcasting organisation. Likewise, coverage of an issue in a manner which the government and Dáil may define as likely to promote crime or lead to disorder, may lead to direct censorship — thus the existing prohibitions on interviews not only with members of illegal organisations but with Sinn Fein. Indeed the coverage of the conflict in Northern Ireland has been almost entirely absent from current affairs programmes over the past ten years.

The desire to limit the independence of broadcasters, may, ironically, be greater the more successful the programme is in terms of attracting an audience. With some fluctuations, current affairs programmes on RTE have, since the mid sixties, been highly successful in gaining a large share of the audience — despite the attractions offered on other channels. It has consistently held a prime-time slot, ensuring not only a wide general audience but also its assiduous viewing by the political parties — a group who have never been slow to launch complaints.

The personality system of a small group of tried and trusted presenters is one way in which the broadcasting organisation can attempt to ensure that 'due care' is maintained. However, a well-established personality system characterised by professionalism and authoritativeness, may not only contribute to holding onto the relative independence of the broadcasting organisation but also, possibly, to slowly expanding the extent to which criticism of those in powerful positions is tolerated.

It is not of course only in current affairs that the personality system works — it is endemic throughout television and is one of the primary modes whereby the audience identifies with a programme. The presenter's familiarity, dependability and populism is essential in forging this identification. This is reaffirmed by the regularity of their appearances, the highly ritualised programme sets, formats and introductory sequences, the immediacy of the close-up, the directness of their address to us — the audience, and the repetitiveness of their style

—frequently integrating authoritative, populist and paternalistic elements. In current affairs, presenters can use the tendency of the audience to identify with them to bolster their own authority to speak for us the viewers, and to hold their own in the light of elite criticism.

Current affairs on television is constructed around personalities: not only the personality system of presenters but also the personalities of elite representatives and that tiny minority of non-elite (often 'problem group') members invited to participate in programmes. The close-up of the face is one of its main televisual forms — whether the close-up of the presenter introducing and framing the programme directly to camera, questioning, stimulating and yet containing conflict, orchestrating interventions, policing turn-taking and pacing the discussion, or the close-up of the politician, the trade unionist, the drug addict, the worried and troubled faces of members of 'problem groups'.

In studio discussions constructed around a controversial issue, a cental story-line lies in who wins. Who in this game of wits between protagonists, filmed in close-up, can take the chair's questions and turn them to their own advantage? Who can pace the interview or discussion to ensure their own point is the final one? Who can do these without appearing hostile or aggressive? Who appears in 'reaction-shots' unruffled and yet responsive even under pressure? Who can listen attentively to 'hard' questions from the presenter and not appear dismissive, but reformulate them to suit: the "Yes, but . . ." response? While this form of studio discussion and interview has produced many hours of popular television in the past, one might wonder how long it can continue, given the increasing sophistication of some politicians in manipulating this game and in undermining the chairperson's role, not least by remaining unruffled by his/her 'hard' questions and thus perhaps pressurising the chair to become more aggressive. This of course undermines the audience's identification with the chair, switching it to the 'underdog' under attack, who now may become the 'good guy'. While part of current affairs own rationale has been to be a thorn in the estabishment's side, or as Lelia Doolan said of '7 Days': "Mohair-suited gentlemen were damaged",[22] to draw on populist anti-elite and 'agin-the-government' sentiments, it would now appear that many of the mohair suited may have begun to turn the tables, to learn the art of successful television self-presentation, and in 'trial-by-television' to win out as 'real', 'genuine' and 'honest'.

Despite this encroachment into the presenters' preserve, the current affairs programme is still very much the presenters' world: face-to-face with the viewers, they 'explain' the world to us: articulate and terse they order and simplify what often appears chaotic and unmanageable, the disordered world is fashioned into a story which makes 'good television', which confirms the programme's and presenter's authority, and which holds audience interest. These characteristics of a 'good story' push it towards articulating known values, ideas which are shared by sufficiently large and powerful elites, what has been called the ideological 'middle ground'.

Presenters must not appear too extreme in their views, too 'unrealistic', 'unreasonable' or biased in favour of particular sectional interests. To play the role of 'neutral arbiter' between contending groups, they must themselves appear detached. The establishment of this detached and neutral role is aided by drawing on societal values to which there is widespread — if vague — assent: a belief in parliamentary democracy, in honest government, in the importance of public opinion, in the need for sectional interests to work together for the national good of economic development, in 'concern' for problem groups and the belief that something should be done about them. Current affairs programmes articulate and symbolically represent in televisual terms these values. Current affairs also, however, symbolically represent the existing class, elite and gender structure by repeatedly giving a tiny minority the right of access to the airwaves, to the exclusion of the vast majority. Indeed when non-elites appear they tend either to be as 'representatives' of problem groups or as an occasional 'vox-pop' chorus most frequently used to echo and confirm the presenters' interpretation of the topic in hand.[23]

If current affairs programmes do influence public opinion, it is unlikely to move it in any radically new direction. It is locked into the existing value system by twin and interdependent characteristics of its personality system and its need to articulate the middle ground, characteristics which are themselves influenced by the social, political and economic contexts within which RTE works.

REFERENCES

1. Maurice Gorham, *Forty Years of Irish Broadcasting,* Dublin, 1967, p. 203
2. Jack White, *RTV Guide,* January 12, 1962.
3. Broadcasting Authority Act, 1960, Sec. 18 (1).
4. Quoted in Lelia Doolan et al., *Sit Down and Be Counted,* Dublin, 1969, p. 91.
5. Todd Andrews, *Man of No Property,* Dublin, 1982. p. 271.
6. See for example, Anthony Smith (ed), *Television and Political Life, Studies in Six European Countries,* London, 1979; and, with regard to election broadcasting, Mary Kelly, "Influences on Broadcasting Policies for Election Coverage", in Jay Blumler (ed), Communicating to Voters, *Television in the First European Parliamentary Elections,* London, 1983.
7. It may be noted that the 'personality system' is endemic throughout television, as can be seen in the importance of groups of well-known 'newscasters', of 'the host' on light entertainment and sports programmes, the 'quiz master' etc. The importance of this system as well as the differences between it and the 'star system' in films are discussed in, John Langer, "Television's Personality System", in *Media Culture and Society,* Vol. 4, 1981, pp. 351-365.
8. Lelia Doolan et al. op. cit., p. 82.
9. Ibid., p. 86.
10. Kishan Kumar, "Holding the Middle Ground: the BBC, the Public and the Professional Communicator", in James Curran et al. (eds), *Mass Communication and Society,* London, 1977, p. 239.
11. Ibid., p. 244.

12. Charlotte Brunsdon and David Morley, *Everyday Television: 'Nationwide'*, London, 1978, p. 9.

13. For development of this theme see John Langer, op. cit.

14. Ibid., p. 357.

15. Ibid., p. 361.

16. Stuart Hall et al., 'The Unity of Current Affairs Television', in *Working Papers in Cultural Studies,* Spring, 1976, p. 68.

17. Fine Gael, *Working Through to a Just Society,* Dublin, 1971.

18. On the percentage of female producers and presenters on current affairs programmes in 1980, see *Report to the Radio Telefís Éireann Authority, Working Party on Women in Broadcasting,* Dublin, 1981.

19. See Bill Roche, "Social Partnership and Political Control: Strategy and Industrial Relations in Ireland", in Mary Kelly et al. (eds), *Power, Conflict and Inequality,* Dublin, 1982.

20. See Paul Bew and Henry Patterson, *Seán Lemass and the Making of Modern Ireland,* 1945-66, Dublin, 1982.

21. The capacity of trade unions to manage their own internal affairs without legal sanctions has been constantly stressed by trade union representatives on current affairs programmes: e.g., 'Frontline', 18 December 1979 and 'Public Account', 4 February 1981.

22. Lelia Doolan, op. cit.

23. For use of vox pop as a chorus to reinforce the presenter's words see Mary Kelly, "Television Elections as Ritual, The Case of the European Elections", in Chris Curtin et al., *Culture and Ideology in Ireland,* Galway (1984).

5   The Late Late Show, *Controversy and Context*

Maurice Earls

Choosing the *Late Late Show* as a subject of study is unlikely to cause surprise given that the social role of the programme has been a matter of public interest since its inception. However, apart from Gay Byrne's book *To Whom It Concerns,* no detailed observations on the show have been published. Perhaps this is because conclusions drawn from the study of public opinion and the factors which influence it are often tenuous. Ultimately an analysis can only be accepted if an integrated counter analysis cannot be mounted against it. Cultural history is far from an exact science, and the purpose of this paper is, chiefly, to contribute to a debate on the socio-political role and context of the *Late Late Show* over the past twenty years.

The study of the programme is rendered difficult as so few examples of it remain on file. For instance, none of the controversial shows from the 1960s are available. Fortunately, this is not as major a handicap as it might appear. Because the show has been at the top of the TAM ratings for 20 years, the public are deeply familiar with its format and its presenter. Furthermore, the public debate which followed controversial issues of the programme did not occur, nor was it reported in any detail, on the programme itself. The press, on the other hand, which is available for consultation, took part in and reported such debates.

The general familiarity with the programme and the existence of newspaper records facilitates a relatively organised study despite the absence of the programmes themselves. This paper, however, does not aspire to an even concentration over the show's twenty years. The controversies of the 1960s receive more attention, because the public debates which followed were far more extensive than any which occurred in the seventies. Within the limits of this methodology the study has yielded some tentative conclusions. In brief, these are that the hostility excited by the programme came chiefly from traditional sources within the political and cultural establishment who resented the emergence of a forum for popular debate which was liberal in bias and outside the control of traditional cultural authority. Secondly, that these traditional views did not represent the values of society at large and that there was considerable public disenchantment with the established outlook and tolerance for more liberal views. Thirdly, it is suggested that Gay Byrne in his attitudes and broadcasting style, enacted many of the changes Irish society was anxious to make. Moreover the decidedly non-subversive, and indeed in many respects conservative, character of his personality was found immensely reassuring by the Irish public who wished to modernize while retaining an overall social stability and cultural identity. The programme and its producer created an atmosphere of liberalism which was historically apposite. This however, did not extend to a social radicalism in respect of property rights. Indeed, Gay Byrne has always shied away from property related issues such as housing or industrial problems.

The *Late Late Show* went on the air in the summer of 1962, six months after the commencement of Irish television. In *To Whom It Concerns* Gay Byrne explained that it was devised to create the ambience of an evening around an Irish country fire with a young master entertaining various guests. This fireside image comes straight from the twilight world of de Valera's ideal Ireland and it is significant that in 1962 the desire for an Irish chat show found expression in the language and imagery of protectionist culture. The programme, of course, did not adhere to the fireside motif. On the contrary, when it was actually broadcast no efforts were made to conceal that it was taking place in a television studio. The *Late Late Show* from the outset, and quite some time before it became a broadcasting fashion in other countries, disdained to hide cameras, lighting equipment, wiring and technicians from public view. In exposing the actual studio components of television broadcasting the programme was identifying with the medium and consciously adopting a modern character.

At first the press did not quite know what to make of the programme with its mixture of serious and casual panellists and guests, its studio audience and its ability to move from serious to light topics and back again without apparent effort. The public, however, were less at a loss and watched the programme in large numbers from the beginning. By the end of its first season the mood of the press had changed and it was generally acknowledged to be a success.

The *Late Late Show* was popular because it was lively. And it was lively because it was modern and post-protectionist in its style. The country's intellectuals and creative thinkers were still deeply enmeshed in the cultural values and language of de Valera's Ireland. Even the initiators of the *Late Late Show,* who were clearly trying to do something new, were conceptually confined through the influence of that ideology. The ideology of self-sufficiency was arguably in its day a modernizing force in Irish society. By the early sixties it was, however, a failed god and the public had grown impatient with its unyielding cultural dogma. The *Late Late Show* which operated outside the grammar of established values was to become, at once, an outlet for popular impatience and an example of what it might be possible for an outward looking and modern Ireland to achieve.

1966 was undoubtedly the year the *Late Late Show* came of age as an agent of controversy. The first incident that year concerned Victor Lownes, an executive of the playboy empire, who was visiting Ireland and whom it was proposed to invite onto the programme. Lownes, it seems, attempted a little media manipulation by issuing statements to the press before the invitation was finalized, to the effect that he was appearing and that the purpose of his visit was to recruit Irish girls to work in playboy clubs in Britain. The culture of independent Ireland attached a high premium to sexual restraint, particularly in women, and had a particularly low regard for England in the area of sexual conduct and morals. In this context Victor Lownes was inevitably seen as something of an English Count Dracula come to prey on Ireland's comely maidens.

The making of a major controversy may be discerned from the style of the press reports in the days before the show was due to be broadcast. However, Telefís Éireann cut short this potential controversy by issuing a statement to the effect that they had not been aware of the purpose of Mr. Lownes' visit but that when this had become clear the invitation was withdrawn. It seems unlikely that the *Late Late Show* would have facilitated Lownes in his self-publicity. If it had, however, there can be little doubt that a major row would have followed which might well have proved terminal for the show. In this matter Telefís and the *Late Late Show* displayed a sympathy with its critics which was to be a recurring feature of the controversies engendered by the programme. If the producers of the show were crusaders they were also pre-eminently survivalists.

The following month the programme was again the centre of attention. This time criticism centred on a game which was played with volunteer participants from the audience.[1] At one point a woman was asked the colour of her nightdress on her wedding night. The Bishop of Clonfert initiated the public controversy which followed and the affair duly became known as the Bishop and the Nightie incident. The Bishop protested vigorously at the inclusion of such a question and his objections were soon taken up by others. Under the heading of "Bishop calls *Late Late Show* objectionable" the *Irish Times* reported the Bishop's sermon on the following Monday as follows:

> *I regret having to commence my sermon today with a vigorous protest against the contents of the Late Late Show on Telefís*

Eireann last night. Many of you, I am sure, will have seen the programme; the fewer the young people that saw it the better.

I know you will all agree with me when I describe it as most objectionable. I am referring to certain morally — or rather immorally — suggestive parts of the show, which were completely unworthy of Irish television, unworthy of Irish producers, unworthy of Irish audiences for whom the programme was destined, unworthy of a public service which is being maintained by public monies contributed in taxes by Irish people [sic].

Surely Irish television is capable of producing, at least, less debasing and less disgraceful entertainment; surely, if we want to look at television, we are entitled to see a programme that is more in keeping with moral standards traditional in our Catholic country.

I have registered my protest; I ask you to do the same, in any manner you think fit, so as to show the producers in Irish television that you, as decent Irish Catholics, will not tolerate programmes of this nature.[2]

The Bishop's objection was in a long and well established tradition. The problem from the point of view of a traditional Catholic outlook was that the offence given was very slight, and that a process of economic and social modernization had reduced the public inclination to reject everything with a sexual reference. In his book *To Whom It Concerns* Gay Byrne says that of the phone calls received by the station on the night the programme was broadcast only one objected to the morality of the question.[3] In its criticism of the show the *Catholic Standard* reflected the new mood: "Nothing very demoralizing or dangerous took place, but what shocking bad taste".[4]

This view of the matter is quite a distance from the assertion that it was unfit for Irish audiences and unfit for Irish television. In general the tone of the letters to the press in support of the Bishop was closer to that of the *Catholic Standard's* reviewer than to that of the Bishop's original protest. One *Evening Press* reader, who reflected the mood of those inclined to sympathise with the Bishop, accepted that the incident was a "little vulgar" but added that:

...in the context of Irish modern amusements it was normal and far less gross than what we see and hear in the picture houses and in the theatres. In other words Dr. Ryan is out of touch with ordinary everyday Irish life. This, I feel, is the vital element in the Late Late Show incident.[5]

There were also, of course, many letters to the papers making a similar point but without expressing any sympathy for the Bishop.

However, a Bishop was, and remained, an important figure of the establishment, and his utterances, however archaic, could not be dismissed lightly by that establishment. Loughrea town commissioners congratulated the Bishop on his protest over the show. One speaker, expressing the mood of the meeting said of the *Late Late Show:* "It is a dirty programme that should be abolished altogether".[6] The Mayo G.A.A. also protested as did the Meath Vocational Education Committee which complained of the show on the grounds of "mediocrity, anti-national tone and recently low moral tone".[7] Numerous other similar bodies around the country complained in the same manner. Stephen Barrett, T.D. wrote to the press:

> *"From Press reports I understand that part of the entertainment offered to viewers of the Late Late Show on Saturday night consisted of questioning a husband and wife, in the absence of each other, about the colour of the nightdress worn by the lady on her honeymoon, some years ago.*
>
> *"Mr. Gay Byrne, the compere, appears to consider such intimate discussion in public as being quite normal and acceptable. He is in fact 'absolutely at a loss to know why there should be any objections from anybody.'*
>
> *"It is possible, however that a large number of viewers do not share Mr. Byrne's morbid curiosity in regard to the colour of Mrs. Fox's honeymoon nightie. In many homes such a discussion is not usually engaged in and to have it thrust into the midst of family and friends can, to some of us at all events, appear to be in utter bad taste.*
>
> *"The question put to Mr. and Mrs. Fox on Saturday night was, to say the least of it, an intimate one, the answer to which was not calculated to interest any ordinary adult person."*
>
> *"Possibly with the passage of time Mr. Gay Byrne's mind will become more enlightened on the sort of entertainment calculated to meet with objection. In the absence of such a desirable development it is possible that his Saturday night feature in the foreseeable future might become known as the Late Late Late Show. Many of his viewers are grown up and Mr. Byrne should attempt to reach their stature.*
>
> *Stephen D. Barrett, T.D.,*
> *Dail Eireann,*
> *Dublin 2.*[8]

In the Seanad the episode gave rise to a more wide ranging debate during which J. B. Quigley declared in relation to media personalities such as Gay Byrne:

> *"...one of the most annoying things is that you have a fellow on a programme and some fellow on another programme starts praising him up and the personality is born. Like Krushchev, I am all against the cult of the personality."*

The same speaker objected, in significant terms, to drink advertisements:

"I think it is improper and a trifle disgusting to see a young girl taking a glass of brown ale in her hand and this is presented as the norm for teenagers. I would like to have some episcopal pronouncement on this."[9]

Many leading figures of the political establishment of the 1960s were removed from the rhetoric and values of these protests. Sean Lemass's cabinet, supposedly the youngest in Europe, was beginning to follow through at a social and political level on the implications of the Lemass/Whitaker initiative of opening the economy to foreign investment in the late fifties. In this they had extensive public support and the mood of the period was one of conscious modernising. However, conservative values were deeply ingrained particularly amongst those public figures who did not identify with the Lemass programme and its implications. These values provided the rhetoric for the condemnatory response to phenomena such as the *Late Late Show*. It would necessarily be some time before the cultural implications of the new economic departure would be fully articulated or accepted. In these circumstances members of the Lemass cabinet were careful to choose the area in which they contested the traditional outlook, as in the case of Brian Lenihan's relaxation of censorship and George Colley's public disagreement with the Bishop of Galway over rural education. Modernising politicians were not prepared to be drawn on controversies generated by the *Late Late Show* and remained silent on the Bishop and the Nightie incident.

The advocates of a traditional outlook had a monopoly of establishment comment on the incident. Following a deluge of criticism from such sources the Telefis Eireann authorities decided to apologise. Gay Byrne, after initially expressing surprise over the Bishop's protest, associated himself with the apology.

The letters published in the press on the subject divided fairly evenly for and against the Bishop. An interesting feature, as has been noted, was that the support of many who favoured the Bishop fell short of total approval. This pattern was particularly evident in the letters of support written by individuals. However, it is not found at all in the statements issued by Vocational Education Committees, County Councils, town commissioners and other similar bodies whose tone was one of virulent opposition to the *Late Late Show* and unqualified support for the Bishop. An examination of the reasons for this divergence of tone does not fall within the scope of this essay. However, it can perhaps be said that the show's critics represented the instinctive voice of Irish conservatism. Their readiness to criticise the *Late Late Show* and RTE — which persists into the 1980s — is evidence that the medium in general and the programme in particular are perceived as being at odds with the Irish conservative view of the world.

In evaluating the social significance of the *Late Late Show* and its ability to survive numerous difficulties, consideration of Gay Byrne's role and personality is unavoidable. There was something in his approach which linked him to the liberal mood of the period but at the same time enabled him to escape from the programme's critics in one piece.

Gay Byrne is not an intellectual in that he has little taste for the abstract. He has attitudes on a wide range of subjects but he does not abstract general principles or a political position from them. Attitudes are more flexible and less distinct than principles by their nature, and his preference in this area has undoubtedly facilitated his survival. The heavy weight of a worked-out set of principles would have been a considerable cargo to carry across the treacherous ground of Irish social politics over the past twenty years. The *Late Late Show* and Gay Byrne, thus unencumbered, made it successfully and in the process, perhaps unwittingly, functioned as something of a mid-wife to contemporary Irish liberalism.

If Gay Byrne was not particularly concerned with questions of principle, the attitudes he brought to the *Late Late Show* as presenter and producer were far from ideologically neutral. In *To Whom It Concerns* he wrote:

> *"We lived in Ireland (and still do to a very great extent) in a very protective, paternalistic society where our elders and betters — notably the politicians and the clergy — decided for us what we should be told and what should be kept from us; what we were capable of assimilating and what could only disturb our tranquil existence and cause us worry and annoyance. I had realised for many years that those who administered Radio Eireann were most conscious of this aspect of their stewardship — not in any vicious, underhand way, but with a very conscientious and dedicated realisation of the power they had and of the responsibility which went with running a national radio service. The result was that as far as many people of my generation were concerned, our national radio service was, simply, an irrelevancy, an elite organisation run by an elite for an elite, where the right people got the right jobs in order to perpetuate a certain ethos...they were of a certain mould and therefore could be relied upon to have predictable attitudes to matters of language, outlook, nationalism and what was acceptable and what was not."*[10]

Gay Byrne came to adulthood as a young man who was somewhat outside of and critical of the cultural establishment. It was this circumstance which equipped the presenter of the *Late Late Show* for his role in the initiation of public debate which was outside the terms of reference of Irish society's traditional outlook.

In the extract from *To Whom It Concerns* reference is made to "those of my generation" who shared the feelings described. Gay Byrne knew there was an audience for programmes which went beyond the ethos of

Radio Eireann. He was not surprised or offended when the programme became a vehicle for liberal opinion. Arguably the relative failure of such figures as Bunny Carr and Frank Hall who stood in for Gay Byrne on occasion, and who were not divorced from the cultural establishment, should be seen in this context.

If Gay Byrne had been a militant liberal or secularist with a predictable and unyielding view on every subject that came up for discussion he, too, would have been unsuccessful. He was successful because his liberalism was moderate and undogmatic, and co-existed with an obvious respect for institutions and individuals who were clearly not liberal. In this he reflected the mood of the time, which wished to change the direction of Ireland's efforts to achieve economic well-being without entirely rejecting the status quo. The new departure would involve an outward-looking society seeking prosperity through contacts abroad, as opposed to the earlier model for prosperity through self-sufficiency.

The culture of the comfortable homestead and turf fire associated with the ideology of the protectionist economy was, of course, inappropriate to the changes underway. Gay Byrne had experienced Ireland of the 1950s with its huge emigration and falling population. He was part of the generation which rejected as inadequate the idea of self-sufficiency. The often frail cultural structures of the new state were, of necessity, deeply enmeshed in this philosophy of protectionism. However, there were great dangers attached to rejecting the cultural character taken on by independent Ireland. If the ethos which had developed with the struggle for political autonomy was rejected with the failed policy of self-sufficiency the whole point and validity of independence would be called into question. It was essential to maintain a positive attitude towards existing Irish values while moving towards the more liberal cultural values of the outside world with whom Ireland was determined to trade.

Gay Byrne achieved this on the *Late Late Show*. He facilitated the introduction of liberal ideas to the public without an abrupt rejection of the existing culture. Arguably his achievement on the *Late Late Show* was actually greater than successfully maintaining this duality of attitude. If Ireland as an open economy was to be successful it was neccesary for it to develop a specifically Irish culture compatible with and integrated with its economic practice. The *Late Late Show* was the first and perhaps most significant achievement yet in this category. When people turned on their television sets and saw Gay Byrne chatting easily to all sorts of exotic foreigners on terms of evident equality while still being a nice young Dubliner it augmented the confidence and hope with which the public increasingly viewed national prospects in the 1960s.

People with something dissident to say felt relatively comfortable on the *Late Late Show*. They knew the presenter was carrying no banners for the Church, the G.A.A., the Irish language or any other pillars of the establishment. Dissident elements who aspired to a more cosmopolitan culture than that dominant in the overwhelmingly agricultural Irish economy had existed for a long time. However, the continued decline of the population after independence which reached alarming proportions during the economically stagnant fifties had the effect of spreading cultural doubt. As the doubt spread a new optimism also developed, as has been noted, which welcomed the Lemass economic programme and believed in the possibility of Irish modernization and development. It was this audience which carried the *Late Late Show* to the top of the TAM ratings, and moreover, which recognised in the programme a specifically Irish cultural achievement which did not look in on itself but out, with confidence, towards the rest of the world.

The mood of the 1960s gave rise to a specifically Irish liberalism. The public did not want those whose liberalism was British or European in character to establish the terms of the new phase in Irish history. The government minister who was author of the celebrated complaint against "political queers from Trinity College" perhaps crudely reflected the widespread desire for a popular Irish character to the developments underway. The second Vatican Council and the visit to Ireland of John F. Kennedy, which were undoubtedly amongst the most significant cultural events of the 1960s, were both perceived in the context of this desire for an Irish modernity. In international terms Kennedy was perceived as young, go-ahead and modern. In Ireland the crucial gloss put on this was that he was a Catholic of Irish ancestry. He was thus a symbol of what Ireland wished to become in the 1960s. Similarly the Vatican Council proposed far reaching changes for the Church which was, of course, to remain one hundred per cent Catholic. It too, then, was a symbol of the country's more general ambitions and became the ideological focus for the new generation of Irish liberals.

Gay Byrne also fitted into this pattern. The presenter of the show did not grow up a bohemian, critical of all elements within the dominant culture. He was educated by the Christian Brothers in Synge Street and while his experience in school and in the Dublin of the 1950s did not firmly attach him to traditional values, he was in many respects a conservative young man. He wished to see the country modernise, but without large scale disruption. The audience of the *Late Late Show* found his essential loyalty to the status quo reassuring and he too became something of a symbol for Ireland's desire to modernise. While great pride was taken in his easy mastery of the modern skill of television broadcasting he was also perceived as being committed to Irish broadcasting and to Ireland, a commitment epitomized by his return to Ireland from Britain.

Before leaving the subject of Gay Byrne's affect on the programme an important and somewhat discordant aspect of his influence should be mentioned. While the impromptu character of the *Late Late Show* was central to its popularity there was always a certain tension between that feature of the show and its presenter. With experience Gay Byrne

115

developed an extremely high degree of control over the pace and content of the programme. By using his wits and personality, the breaks for entertainment and advertising, by deciding the composition of the panel and by controlling the mixture of guests and the timing of their appearances he achieved a level of control which often belied the show's casual format. The patronising manner in which he often treated the audience reflected his overriding interest in control and efficiency on air. Nevertheless the impromptu element remained structurally present in the show and occasionally overwhelmed the easy control which the presenter had achieved by the seventies. Perhaps the most notable example of this was the celebrated youth issue of the show which achieved near anarchy and revealed a decidedly tetchy side to the host's personality.

The Brian Trevaskis affair followed the Bishop and the Nightie incident in March 1966. The details of this incident are fairly generally known. Briefly, Brian Trevaskis, taking the topical 1916 proclamation as his text, claimed that none of its ideals had been achieved. He took the example of equal rights and equal opportunities and claimed that only the children of the wealthy could afford university education. Money was spent on churches, but little was available for education, he said, adding: "We are sending missionaries all over the world to convert people to Irish christianity. I think it is about time we applied Christianity in our own country".[11] He praised Dr. Noel Browne and criticised the Archbishop of Dublin, Dr. McQuaid, particularly in the context of John McGahern having lost his job as a school teacher for having written a novel which was judged indecent and obscene. He implied that the Christian Brothers were over fond of the cane and described the recently built Galway Cathedral on which one million pounds had been spent as a monstrosity. "I don't blame the people, I would rather blame the Bishop of Galway",[12] he said. He also referred to the Bishop as a moron and questioned the value of the Irish language. Not surprisingly his criticisms were extensively and vehemently rejected.

Most of the objections from individuals, county councils and other similar bodies were confined to simple denunciations of Brian Trevaskis, Gay Byrne and the *Late Late Show*. One of the few efforts to think through the implications of objecting to Mr. Trevaskis's freedom to speak his mind was published in the *Irish Catholic* for April 1966. The TV reviewer of that journal claimed that: "Telefis has the responsibility to define which programmes are suitable for responsible expressions of views of important controversial content and which programmes by their nature are unsuitable for this".[13]

What is being suggested here is a structured and controlled format for the debate of controversial subjects. Moreover, the author implicitly limits free speech on controversial subjects to "responsible expression of views". Brian Trevaskis' view clearly did not fall within this category in the view of the writer who added: "Somebody must decide soon the real function or nature of the *Late Late Show*". If it was to be a structured debate then the rules of impartiality could be insisted on and only the views of the responsible and people of standing and competence would be heard. The *Irish Catholic* emphasised the unstructured context in which Brian Trevaskis's views emerged:

> *"In the programme last week was a panel of writers who were there presumably to talk about their approach to their work. Three of them did so but the fourth took the occasion to launch into his personal opinions on a variety of subjects and a general attack on the Church.... If the Late Late Show is to become a place for expression of views in which selected guests can say what they like then it must be acknowledged and prepared as a serious discussion programme ... there would have to be a chairman who preserves a balance rather than throw in innocuous comments or asides which amount to an uneasy handwashing....If on the other hand it is not intended to be such but to be merely a form of entertainment then it must be so controlled that nobody uses it, no matter how sincerely for soap box oratory."*[14]

While this article represents what is perhaps the most coherent argument in objection to Brian Trevaskis, its various elements were present in a great number of letters to the press, and indeed in newspaper editorials. The problem however, was that a talk show such as the *Late Late Show* could not operate these principles because it was impossible to know exactly what guests would say. On some occasions the debate format was used. However such programmes were clearly a departure from the classic *Late Late Show* style which was characterized by guests who could speak casually on either serious or light topics. Controversy generated by the *Late Late Show* often followed impromptu remarks by guests on serious subjects which were not hedged in by the rhetorical qualifications normally associated with expertise and which were outside the frame of reference of established political divisions.

Arguably, the popularity of the *Late Late Show* owed as much to its casual format as it did to Gay Byrne's style and the general social context. The manner in which serious subjects were discussed on the programme, was, after all, quite similar to the way they were discussed in homes, work-places and pubs in everyday life. The mixture of serious discussion with light entertainment was more representative of everyday discussion than was a pedagogical panel of experts presenting their views in rota according to formal regulations imposed rigorously by a referee. It might be said that in this sense the *Late Late Show* constituted a democratization of opinion which was immensely popular because it came at a time when there was a search underway for a language to represent the aspirations of a new optimism. Guests on the *Late Late Show* gave their opinions as ordinary people, which enabled the audience to take them or leave them. The casual style of the programme did not intimidate the audience which did not feel that it was going against authority by accepting one point against another. However, those who were loyal to the conservative culture which thrived in independent Ireland recognised the tone of the *Late Late Show* as ominous. The programme, however, did reflect the mood of the 1960s more than did the conservatism of its critics, which helps to explain why it was so popular and why its detractors failed to have it stopped.

It is significant that as in the case of the Bishop and the Nightie incident, the letters to the press presented a somewhat different picture to the apparent anti-Trevaskis consensus. The *Evening Press* which like most papers could only publish a fraction of the letters it received on the subject informed its readers that 40% of those received favoured Trevaskis while 60% disapproved. Tom O'Dea, the *Irish Press's* TV critic, added that people tended to write to newspapers when they objected to something more than when they agreed, and that the real picture in terms of public opinion might in fact have been more favourable to Trevaskis.[15]

Brian Trevaskis was an angry young man, and, notwithstanding his impetuosity, a brave one. It is significant that the only indication we have of public opinion suggests that at least 40% of viewers regarded him favourably. If Tom O'Dea's reasonable point is taken into account, the figure would surely be at least 50%. Why did such a large proportion of the audience find such an extensive and unqualified attack on the institutions of the country acceptable? One reason is of course, the change of mood which has already been discussed. A second reason, it might be argued, relates to the terms of his complaint. Brian Trevaskis was not "a political queer from Trinity College", telling the Irish public that everything they had stood for or believed in was rubbish and that the Irish public had betrayed its own ideals, that it had betrayed the ideals of 1916. By emphasising the liberal aspects of the proclamation Trevaskis was effectively linking his liberal perspective with the struggle to establish the state. It was an immensely appealing connection to emerging Irish liberal opinion and helps to explain why so many people were prepared to defend him notwithstanding his having called the Bishop of Galway a moron.

Conor Cruise O'Brien was one of those who discussed the episode on the programme shortly afterwards. He performed effectively and with characteristic sophistication in support of Trevaskis. In the years following Dr. O'Brien functioned as a liberal and perceptive critic of Irish orthodoxy often on the *Late Late Show*. Yet he has not attracted the public support which came to the less sophisticated and hot-headed Brian Trevaskis. It is difficult not to conclude that an important reason for this has been the public association of Dr. O'Brien with the view that the rising of 1916 was in some way wrongheaded. A further reason for the support received by Brian Trevaskis was, arguably, related to the radical Christian terms in which his complaint was couched. This frame of reference rendered his argument sympathetic to indigenous Irish liberalism which was imbued with the radical spirit of the second Vatican Council.

Turning to the question of the *Late Late Show* as a source of social change, it is possible to say that in itself the programme represented a considerable development in Irish mass communication and tended to reflect the social changes and the atmosphere of the 1960s more effectively than other mass media. Perhaps one specific social change can be traced to the programme itself, that of acclimatizing people to hearing points of view with which they did not agree and on subjects outside those sanctioned by the established political divisions. In *To Whom It Concerns* Gay Byrne remarks that by 1972 the Brian Trevaskis outburst would have appeared old hat to most people.[16] Gay Byrne may be overstating his case here. If someone called the Bishop of Galway a moron in 1972 or indeed in 1982 some public controversy would almost certainly have followed.

However, under the influence of the *Late Late Show* and a fairly rapid pace of social development the public became less unsettled by non-traditional points of view and by forums of expression which were not under the influence of the traditional authorities. The taboo which attached to sexual matters declined considerably and the show featured several programmes on sexual topics in the 1970s which led to no great controversy.

In 1972 Gay Byrne, reflecting on the level of hypocrisy in Irish society, remarked that British Sunday newspapers outsold Irish Sunday newspapers in Ireland but that if an Irish Sunday newspaper attempted to publish in the English style it would not be acceptable to the public. In relation to 1966 he is almost certainly right. In relation to 1972, he may also be correct. However, as we know the *Sunday World* was established in the mid-seventies without any great controversy and has thrived in the Irish market since. The acceptance of the *Sunday World* is remarkable because of the widespread association of "smut" and "lewdness" with England. Things which were considered to be "dirty" were traditionally held to be anti-national, and much that has appeared in the *Sunday World* — to which Gay Byrne contributes a column — would have been traditionally regarded as "dirty". The survival and prosperity of this journal is a measure of attitudinal changes in contemporary Ireland. However, a newspaper is a far less formidable medium that a popular television show. Buying a paper is a conscious choice and assimilating its message generally requires the effort of reading. The *Late Late Show*, as so many county councillors observed over the years, comes into everyone's living room and is part of a national service. It is unlikely that such "anti-national" lewdness would have ever been, or would yet be, tolerated as a deliberate aspect of the show.

The programme has, however, acclimatised people to the legitimacy of other opinions and views. One show in the late seventies featured a long and sympathetic interview with an Irish lesbian who described the problems she encountered as a lesbian. One would have thought that this would have greatly offended traditional values, yet there is no trace of controversy in the public press following the show. It seems curious that this issue excited no controversy when in 1966 a light-hearted reference to nudity in the context of orthodox heterosexual relations led to a national controversy and a public apology. There are two factors which should be borne in mind when considering this. First, a traditional figure of authority did not condemn the later show. If a bishop had condemned it, it is likely that those who remained loyal to the authority of the Church would have supported him. Secondly, the discussion was social in emphasis and avoided explicitly sexual references.

By the late 1970s the programme was long acknowledged as a national institution and one which was generally considered to have had a very positive influence on the country. In June 1979 Patrick Moriarty,, the new chairman of RTE articulated a popular attitude towards the show when he said: "I don't think I have missed the *Late Late* once. I think that it has had a very liberalising effect on the country and must be considered in any future social history of Ireland".[17]

The woman who wrote to the *Sunday Independent* saying: "All this amazes me because there have been very definitely *Late Lates* which were insulting and offensive to the majority of Catholics here"[18] was virtually alone in her protest. Patrick Moriarty's views represented the new orthodoxy on the *Late Late Show.*

It would be impossible to conclude these observations without some reference to the Madam Sin controversy of November 1982, which at first sight appears anachronistic and reminiscent of the various furores of the 1960s.

It is difficult and perhaps dangerous to analyse recent social controversy. Nevertheless I believe the Madam Sin episode does tie in with many of the themes raised in this paper. The *Late Late Show* in its structure and content has over the years provided a forum for certain currents of dissident opinion and contributed to the legitimization of such opinion. Nevertheless, it should not be forgotten that traditionalist opinion has, throughout the years of the *Late Late Show,* remained strong and arguably predominant in Irish political and social affairs. In the light of the recent pro-amendment campaign it seems that those adhering to traditional Catholic values have undertaken something of an offensive.

The outburst of letter-writing and complaint over the Madam Sin show should perhaps be seen in the context of traditional elements being in a state of preparedness for battle. Cynthia Payne, a retired English brothel keeper, lent herself to the traditional rhetoric cf Irish complaint. One County Councillor declared typically:

"we saw the scum of Britain on our TV screens. The institution of

marriage was prostituted and sex was portrayed at animal level".[19]

While the county councillors fulminated wildly the letters of complaint to the press generally made more interesting reading. It emerges quite clearly from these letters that many objectors saw the Madam Sin episode as merely one aspect of a deeper problem which concerned the *Late Late Show* and liberal propaganda. In general the more articulate letters of protest focussed on the fact that another English guest on the programme admitted openly that she had had two abortions and defended abortion as a right. This, of course, was the issue on which the traditionalists launched the amendment crusade. Gay Byrne indicated on the programme that the show would be returning to the question. Naturally pro-amendment forces preferred not to have the issue discussed in a forum which had functioned in the liberal interest over 20 years. The howls of outrage which followed the Madam Sin programme were a reflection of the new militant traditionalist lobby which had no reason to like the programme, which was offended by the treatment of brothel-keeping as a legitimate activity and which was reminded by the pro-abortion views of one of the guests that the show was unlikely to be an ally of its crusade.

Gay Byrne and his colleagues must have thought the protest anachronistic. His initial rejection of his critics revealed a considerable confidence. Referring to attacks from pulpits he described as "an interesting theological principle"[20] the recommendation of one priest that parishioners should withhold their licence fees. RTE itself seemed to give early protestors the brush off. A spokeswoman was reported in the *Sunday Press* as having said that the content of the programme was the responsibility of the programme makers. It was up to them to decide who should and who should not appear on programmes.[21] However four days later RTE was reported as having said it was "looking into" the programme and added "Top programme people are speaking to those in charge of the *Late Late Show* office about the matter. They are expressing concern at the type of material which appeared on the programme and we are looking for comments".[22] Shortly afterwards according to Press reports Mr. George Waters unreservedly apologised and associated Gay Byrne with the apology.[23] Gay Byrne refused to comment but someone associated with him is reported to have said "he knew nothing about it and was not apologising".[24] By mid-December the incident had developed further. Mr. Fred O'Donovan, Chairman of the RTE Authority issued a statement to the effect that as the *Late Late Show* was in the entertainment area it would not be allowed to discuss the abortion question.[25] Gay Byrne said that he was appalled by the statement attributed to Mr. O'Donovan but that he had no intention of resigning.[26]

It is clear that the tension which existed between a liberal and traditional outlook in Ireland of the 1960s still exists in the 1980s. The public has become acclimatized to hearing a very wide range of views in the interim, not least on the *Late Late Show* itself. Because of this process of acclimatization the programme could never again achieve the same level of national attention or notoriety after the major controversies of the 1960s. But, as the Madam Sin episode shows, while the public may have grown accustomed to hearing very liberal ideas expressed they were far from established in Irish society. This process has been paralleled by a widespread realization that the open economy has not, as yet, proved a panacea to Ireland's economic ills. The optimism of the 1960s which facilitated the emergence of the *Late Late Show* as a symbol of the changing Ireland and rendered Gay Byrne possibly the most popular man in the country has given way to a calmer realization that the problems of development and modernization cannot be solved at a stroke. This new mood, accentuated by the recessions of the seventies and eighties, is one which is wary of heroes, magic solutions and public symbols. With a highly skilled broadcaster like Gay Byrne producing and presenting the programme, the *Late Late Show* will continue to be popular but it will be an ordinary everyday popularity subject to competition from other programmes.

REFERENCES

1. For details of the incident see *Cork Examiner*, 14.2.66.
2. *Irish Times*, 14.2.66.
3. *To Whom It Concerns*, Gay Byrne, Dublin 1972, p. 75.
4. *Catholic Standard*, 18.2.66.
5. *Evening Press*, 16.2.66.
6. *Ibid.*
7. *Ibid.*
8. *Irish Press*, 16.2.66.
9. *Irish Press*, 16.2.66.
10. *To Whom It Concerns, op. cit.*, p. 57.
11. *Irish Catholic*, 1.4.66.
12. *Ibid.*
13. *Ibid.*
14. *Ibid.*
15. *Evening Press*, 2.4.66.
16. *To Whom It Concerns, op. cit.*, p. 89.
17. *Sunday Independent*, 3.6.79.
18. *Sunday Independent*, 10.6.79.
19. *Cork Evening Echo*, 9.11.82.
20. *Evening Herald*, 9.11.82.
21. *Sunday Press*, 7.11.82.
22. *Irish Times*, 11.11.82.
23. *Evening Press*, 18.12.82.
24. *Ibid.*
25. *Irish Press*, 18.12.82.
26. *Sunday Press*, 19.12.82.

6 The Representation of Women in Irish Television Drama

Barbara O'Connor

This paper explores some aspects of the representation of women in Irish television drama. The relationship between television and Irish society poses a number of questions regarding the representation of women. How have women been represented? Has this representation changed over the twenty-one years in which RTE has been in existence? If so, in what ways have the changes in the position of women in Irish society affected their representation over that period? To answer these questions adequately would require a comprehensive study of television drama over the years and the present paper deals only with a very selective number of dramatic products. However, within this more limited context, I would like to suggest that, in general, the representation of women in drama broadcast by RTE has been regressive in that women have either been less visible, or portrayed in less central roles, more recently than in the past.

Debates on the representation of women in the media in general and on television in particular have been prolific in recent years, partially as a consequence of the development of the women's movement of the '60s. Research on women in television drama has basically been of two kinds. Firstly, content analysis where the focus is on the appearance or non-appearance of women in programmes and, in cases where they are visible, the types of roles which they occupy. Generally the findings indicate either 'symbolic annihilation' of women or representation in ways which are considered inferior e.g. in occupationally limited roles such as housewife, nurse, secretary or model. Secondly, semiology, another form of content analysis, seeks to analyse representation by looking at the meaning of a programme through investigation of form, narrative structure, visual style, textual discourses or some combination of these elements. While the latter approach is theoretically more sophisticated than the former, both methods of analysis concentrate exclusively on aspects of the text and fail to explore factors outside the text when dealing with representation.

In my view, representation is never adequately explored or the meanings of a television programme discovered without reference to the people who actually watch the programme, the socially structured audience. Since, until recently, many feminists writing about women and media assumed an undifferentiated 'mass' audience in which all women were affected in the same (usually negative) way by television, it is important to stress the differential composition of the audience and the probable diversity of responses to television drama.

In this paper, then, I want to suggest, as far as possible, ways in which television drama might engage its audience, specifically its female audience. The inclusion of the audience dimension in the debate on representation is not only theoretically but also politically desirable since it is through this dimension that the ideological role of television can be assessed. In other words, it is important to know who watches what and who is influenced by what? However, since there is almost no detailed empirical evidence on audience response to the programmes which I have selected for the purpose of discussion, I must make do with hypothesising some of the potential responses.

In arguing that the representation of women in Irish television drama has been regressive rather than progressive the point of reference must be the position of women in the Republic of Ireland and the possible social, political and ideological shifts in that position over the last twenty-one years. So a judgement must be made on these changes in order to assess the extent to which they have been reflected in media output. It is not within the scope of this paper to do justice to the wealth of work which is currently being conducted or the liveliness of the debates on the position of women in Irish society.

Fairly baldly, I would maintain that the power relations of women vis-à-vis men have not altered radically. While administrative and legal changes have given recognition to the unequal position of women, their operative effects have yet to become visible in the statistics. (I am indebted to Pauline Jackson for making this point to me.) The limited amount of progress which women have made has not been incorporated in any systematic way into media representations. In fact, not only have these changes not been integrated into home-produced RTE drama but the scope for the portrayal of strong female central characters has become even more limited over the years for reasons which I will discuss later.

To illustrate my arguments I am selecting three particular dramatic productions, *The Riordans, Bracken* and *The Ballroom of Romance. The Riordans* was a long-running home-produced serial which enjoyed top ratings throughout its television lifespan (it has since been transferred to radio). It was first transmitted in 1965 and continued with one episode per week until the beginning of 1979. *Bracken,* a series of twelve episodes, transmitted in two, six-episode parts, was first transmitted in January 1980 and again had a very high viewing audience. *The Ballroom of Romance* adapted from William Trevor's short story of the same name, was a highly-acclaimed television play transmitted on RTE in October 1982 and was a BBC/RTE co-production. The common feature of these three dramas is that they are all located in rural Ireland and ostensibly represent aspects of Irish rural life including the lives and experiences of women who live in the country.

The present discussion is confined to 'rural' drama partly because there is no adequate representation of contemporary urban women despite the fact that one of the major changes in Irish society over the past twenty years has been a large population shift from rural to urban areas and consequent changes in experience, lifestyle and values. The serial *Tolka Row* which ran from 1963 to 1968 was the last, and indeed only, RTE-produced serial to attempt to deal with the experience of urban working-class women. However, it is true that the series *Strumpet City* located in Dublin of 1913 represented working-class women, but I would suggest that this series ignored their oppression as women and foregrounded instead the class oppression of men.

Of the three productions under discussion, I want to suggest that the serial, *The Riordans* has been more radically influential than either *Bracken* or *The Ballroom of Romance* because of the concurrence of two factors:

1. The fact of its form as a serial which is arguably the dramatic genre which influences women most, and:

2. The specific development of the serial form in Ireland during the late sixties and early seventies.

In relation to the potential influence of serials on women the following points may be noted. Serials deal with the day-to-day lives of their characters, their joys and problems — the sphere of human relations. In a capitalist society where there is a split between the public and private domain women are relegated to the private sphere within the home where they deal in the sphere of human relations and are the guardians of the personal and emotional aspects of life. This has consequences for the representation of women in serials, both in terms of their visibility and in terms of the involvement of a female audience in the genre. Women play a highly visible and somethimes central role in the family/community-based serial like *The Riordans, Coronation Street, Crossroads,* etc.

Women also form a large part of the serial audience. It is interesting to note that the 'sister' and predecessor of the serial, the radio soap-opera, was developed specifically for a female audience by the company Proctor and Gamble to advertise their brand of soap powder, hence the name. Women's continuing enjoyment of serials is borne out by research which I am currently conducting and which also shows a marked gender difference in orientation to serial viewing with men displaying a strong antipathy towards them.

Women, particularly housewives, are very often involved in the lives of the women characters represented in serials. These characters are frequently the television characters to whom they can best relate. This is partially due to the parallel between the rhythm of the serial in its use of 'naturalistic time' (i.e. time in the serial parallels chronological time) and the rhythm of the everyday lives of the female audience. Housewives in particular, who are at home during the day structure their day around particular radio and television programmes. They experience a sense of looking forward to the next episode, to what is happening in Leestown this week or in Coronation Street this evening. And the latest events are talked about with friends and neighbours as if Mary Riordan and Hilda Ogden, too, lived just down the road.

In relation to the specific development of the serial in Ireland, the raising of controversial social issues and problems was an integral part of *The Riordans,* which was the longest-running RTE serial. The convergence of two elements — the high visibility of women in the serial in general and in *The Riordans* in particular — and the debates on contentious social issues — led to the opening up of topics which were of particular interest to women at the time. Questions of contraception, desertion, church annulment of marriage and of marriage itself as it affected women, were all thrown up for public debate. A brief extract from a conversation between Maggie and Willie Mahoney to whom she was engaged at the time will illustrate the latter topic:

> Maggie: *'I don't expect you to agree with me on everything, but you seem to have a pattern all worked out and I've got to fit in with it. We'll always be starting from the way you look on marriage. And that's the marriage I hate, with the husband making the rules and the wife obeying them. Everything that I feel should be in the marriage like equality and the right to a career and to plan my family.'*[1]

Dorothy Hobson, from her audience research on the serial *Crossroads* suggests that because these problems are always related to a character in a serial rather than introduced in an abstract way, for example in the form of an 'information' programme, that they have a greater impact on the audience.[2] In *The Riordans* the dramatic peg on which contemporary concerns were hung was the generational difference between the characters, for example Maggie's disagreements with her mother-in-law Mary; the opposing views of Mary and her children regarding the annulment of her daughter Jude's marriage; conflicting ideas on the control and management of the farm between Tom and his son Benjy.

These inter-generational conflicts are not exclusive to *The Riordans,* they also occur in other serials like *Coronation Street, Dynasty,* etc., but they don't appear to have as great an impact. This is probably due to the fact that the younger generation of characters in *The Riordans* are as central as the older generation whereas it has been suggested, and I would agree, that the younger generation of women in *Coronation Street* are not nearly as compelling as their older counterparts.[3] There are a number of reasons for this but one worth mentioning in this context is the importance attached to the younger generation in a situation where the inter-generational inheritance of the family farm is of primary importance. The latter element provides the cut and thrust of arguments in *The Riordans* which is heightened by the extended family where father, mother, son and daughter-in-law live under the one roof. Audiences are probably more amenable to the point of view of the younger characters if they are perceived as stronger rather than weaker.

While resolutions to the problems and issues raised in *The Riordans* (as indeed in other serials) were not particularly radical or feminist, their importance lay in the challenge to the patriarchial status quo which the public airing of these concerns represented. As a case in point, the contraception debate which revolved around Maggie's use of 'the pill' took place at a time when many women in the Republic of Ireland were in a quandary about the use of the contraceptive pill which was one of the 'artificial' methods of contraception proscribed by the Catholic hierarchy. Within the serial the debate takes place against a backdrop of

a)   The primacy of women's reproductive role within marriage and

b)   Women's immersion in Catholic religious ideology.

While Maggie consults the local priest about being on 'the pill', it is his 'liberal' view in allowing for informed conscience which re-assures her and presents a solution to her problem. But what is at issue here is not the resolution of the contraceptive issue for Maggie but rather the public representation of a non-traditional woman's viewpoint which effectively broke the silence on what had hitherto been one of the taboo areas for Irish women. And equally important, I would think, was the fact that the silence was broken by a well-known and well-liked character who was regarded by the audience as a fairly ordinary decent married woman and not by what they might have regarded as a 'raving feminist' on an 'information' programme.

Public representation of this kind is vital since one of the major forms of oppression operates through the burial of women's experience and its denial to public discourse within the prevailing ideological order. This is particularly applicable to the Republic of Ireland where the suppression of information in the form of censorship had a long and virulent history and where the Censorship of Publications Act (1929) specificially proscribed literature on contraception and abortion. As the women's movement well recognises, the initial part of the fight to change women's lives entails the development of solidarity through the recognition of common experiences and problems. *The Riordans,* I would suggest, acted to some extent as a vehicle for female discourse by engaging with issues which were relevant to women's lives in a way which was both critical and accessible.

Women did not enjoy the same centrality in the series *Bracken* where the two central protagonists are men. In fact women are marginalised within the series, being portrayed either as objects in a sexual capacity or as pawns in a power struggle between the male characters. While the story is located in a rural community, the main narrative thrust is 'the struggle for survival of an obstinate and ambitious young man in a tough farming background'.[4] Although the title of the series would seem to suggest the representation of community life, *Bracken* being short for Kilbracken, the portrayal of community life is largely absent. There is some co-operation in the tasks of sheep farming but this is exclusively a male domain. There is little representation of community life in the traditional sense of portraying a number of families who operate on the basis of co-operation and consensus. It is interesting to note that the two families portrayed in *Bracken,* the Dalys and the Byrnes are, in fact, fraught with tensions and conflicts. Since both the traditional family and community are absent women as central figures are also absent.

One illustration of the differences in the representation of women in *The Riordans* and in *Bracken* is the way in which women's relationship to work is represented. In *The Riordans* Mary and Maggie are regularly shown going about their daily work routine. Admittedly much of their work involves serving their husbands and families and falls within women's traditional role of performing unpaid labour in the domestic sphere. However, there are residues of the family as an economic unit and Maggie works outside the house in the farmyard. Most of the other women in the serial are also shown to be in some way engaged in production and reproduction. Alternatively, the *Bracken* women are, for the most part, ladies of leisure whom we see dawdling through the meadows, reading on the garden swing or departing to or returning from some native or foreign metropolis. In fact Louise's sole contribution to physical labour is to provide a meal for Pat Barry and herself as a prelude to a cosy evening together in his cottage.

Differences also manifest themselves in the representation of the relationship between the sexes. In both *Bracken* and *The Ballroom of Romance* there is a pronounced objectification of women as leisure for men. A typical conversation between Pat and Miley in *Bracken* ends with the following remark:

> Pat: Would you fancy the mother? (Referring to Jill Daly).
> Miley: Wouldn't say 'no'. (laughs).

In *The Ballroom of Romance* there is a similar conversation between Tim Daly and 'Eyes' Horgan in the bar after a period of silent drinking:

> Tim: I wonder is there any talent there tonight? (Referring to the dance).

Eyes:	The same talent there always is. Could you want for better?
Tim:	You could want for it to be obliging.
Eyes:	You're a holy bloody terror, Tim.
Tim:	After seven days work wouldn't you have a right to relaxation, isn't that a fact, Mr. Carey?

Sexist humour is an aspect of all three productions. In all three there are jokes and snide remarks about women but the joking in *The Riordans* is much more gentle and must be viewed in the light of the viewers' build up of knowledge of the characters over time, where remarks are often known by the audience to be made in the context of concealed affection. For instance in the beginning of one episode there is an interchange between Batty Brennan and Michael Riordan joking about Minnie's (Batty's wife) role as village gossip, but later in the same episode we see Batty dissolving in tears in public when he hears that Minnie, who is ill in hospital, has taken a 'turn for the worse'. (The converse could also be argued of course i.e., that because the sexism is more integrated into *The Riordans* than *Bracken* that it is less visible to the audience and therefore operates in a way which is less rather than more critical of patriarchial ideology. These potentially opposing readings highlights the speculative nature of the analysis of representations in the absence of empirical audience research.)

Differences in perceptions of sexuality can also be noted between the productions. In *Bracken* there is a move away from the moral (Catholic) stance on sexuality of *The Riordans* to a more secular, ostensibly liberated view of female sexuality. But while *Bracken* women are certainly more concerned with their own sexual needs the representation of sexuality in *Bracken* isn't any more progressive than in *The Riordans.* Ultimately their sexuality is even more exploited because of their general role within the series as pawns in the power struggle between the two male protagonists; their portrayal as objects rather than subjects. The motif of women as sexual objects is also foregrounded in *The Ballroom of Romance* where the 'preferred reading' would appear to highlight the repression of both male and female sexuality. The oppression of women is particularly highlighted by the manner in which the male characters talk about and treat the women which is exemplified in sexual innuendo and joking, and boisterous rollicking round the dance floor etc. However, this reading is subverted, I would suggest, by the final scene where Bridie goes 'into the field' with 'Bowser' Egan, when it has been made perfectly clear earlier in the film that his advances are repugnant to her. Bridie's final response is to succumb to her fate as the chosen recipient of 'Bowser's' clumsy gropings.

The Ballroom of Romance is one of the most recent dramatic representations of Irish women and warrants some comment because this is a play in which the central character, Bridie, is represented in an extremely sensitive and sympathetic way. The quiet desperation of a country woman working simultaneously in the home, on the land, and looking after an aged parent is foregrounded. However, although Bridie's problems and endurance are foregrounded, her situation is seen as inevitable — "You cannot change the way things are, Bridie", says one of her companions. This resignation to fate is a recurrent motif and the film is narratively closed in Bridie's resigning herself to her fate. There is some evidence to suggest that the setting of the film in the past (the film version of the story is set in the 1950s) coupled with its geographical location in one of the most remote parts of the west of Ireland, distances it from its contemporary female audience who tend to relegate it to another time, another place rather than draw parallels with their own situation today. As part of a research project in which I am currently engaged, a video of *The Ballroom of Romance* is shown to groups of women followed by a group discussion on their reactions to the programme. The analysis is in its initial stages but the following responses are suggestive. Many women placed the film historically and sociologically by references to some of the influences on Irish society during the 1950s (poverty, unemployment, massive emigration, etc.) but these historical forces were seen as pertaining to the past rather than the present. Some women did draw parallels between women's oppression then and now but (and again this is tentative) this was more common among middle-class women than working-class groups. It is also interesting to note that many working-class women in the groups hadn't seen the film when it was originally broadcast on television: some had switched channels when it appeared on screen as it didn't correspond to their notions of what good television entertainment should be, i.e. that it was too slow moving and lacking in a storyline and in dramatic suspense (they were 'waiting for something to happen'). It was also seen as being very limited in scope because it was confined to the ballroom and they wanted to see more of what was going on in the characters' homes. It appears then that the female audience for this type of one-off play could be confined largely to middle-class women.

In the foregoing I have argued that the serial *The Riordans* has given women a more important role in representation than either *Bracken* or *The Ballroom of Romance*. Returning now to the wider context of the debate regarding the relationship between the representation of women by RTE over the last twenty-one years and the position of women in the social structure, I would maintain that women have had a more central and progressive role in the earlier days of television drama than they have had more recently. There are, no doubt, some very interesting productions like the film *Maeve* but they are very thin on the ground. This lack of progress is not necessarily due to a male conspiracy to keep strong women off the screen but is rather due to the conditions of production within RTE, particularly the economic constraints on drama production in recent years.

Serials like *The Riordans* involve high production costs with little chance of recouping finance through export. An alternative source of

130

serials is the US from which serials like *Dallas, Dynasty, Falcon Crest* and *Flamingo Road* can be imported relatively cheaply at a small fraction of the production cost. Ratings for these imported serials are very high and because of the astounding success of these pre-packaged products, their formulaic style is repeated in home-produced drama (as witnessed in *Bracken*). It is difficult to assess the ideological effect of such serials but it is true to say that the women are extremely stereotyped, and live in luxurious surroundings enjoying leisured lifestyles very far removed from the experience of most real women.

The current financial crisis in RTE also necessitates sharing the costs of drama production with other individuals or organisations, usually another broadcasting company or independent film maker. This method of offsetting the increasing costs of drama production has become very popular recently. In the case of co-productions with a foreign broadcasting company RTE have been the initiators of two series — *The Year of the French* (with FR3) and *Caught in a Free State* (with Channel 4). The series *An Irish R.M.* (with Channel Four) and *Ballroom of Romance* (with BBC) were initiated by other broadcasting partners. It could be argued that the aspects of Irish life which appeal to foreign media companies for dramatic reconstruction are characterised by a preference for the past (divorced from connections with the present) often concentrating on the heroic or epic historical events. Since women have been written out of this kind of history this selectivity limits the range of dramatic imagery available to women. In front of me at the moment are two presentation slide packs containing twelve slides each from *The Year of the French* and *Caught in a Free State*. A woman appears in only one of the twenty-four; she is lying in bed in the arms of a bearded gentleman and the accompanying caption states "Kate Cooper 'entertains' McCarthy"!.

In this paper I am not attempting a reversal of 'high culture' theories by proposing an immutable, socio-political scale of television drama ranging from the serial through the series to the 'serious' television play with the serial at the top of the scale and the 'serious' television play at the bottom. There is obviously no necessary causal link between a particular television form and its ideological content. But I am suggesting that there is a link between television form and the purchase it will have on particular sections of the audience under specific socio-historical conditions. Class and gender are two crucial factors in the construction of the audience. Charlotte Brunsdon argues that soap-opera (and serials) requires a viewer who is competent in the codes of personal relations in the domestic sphere or, in other words, must have a particular form of cultural capital; in this case the ability to predict the range of possible consequences attendant upon actions in the spheres of the domestic and familial. Current affairs programmes address a viewer who is competent in the codes of parliamentary democracy and economics.[5] My own research findings corroborate Brunsdon's on differential gender response to these two forms. While class structures the television audience, gender is over-determinant in relation to serials and soap-opera. The majority of women regularly watch and enjoy serials. At the moment, then, the most appropriate dramatic form in which to reach women of all classes is the serial and perhaps the series since the one-off play has little purchase on working-class women. I feel that the insertion of politically progressive ideas into this traditional form can be a starting point towards the development of new forms. It is constantly argued that the only possible radical or consciousness-raising drama must break totally with traditional forms. I would dispute this and would maintain that representation which hopes to be politically effective must take as its starting point the cultural experiences and aesthetic sensibilities of the most marginalised group in television representation, i.e. working-class women.

REFERENCES

1. Wesley Burrowes, *The Riordans,* Gilbert Dalton, Dublin 1977.

2. Dorothy Hobson *Crossroads: The Drama of a Soap Opera,* Methuen, London 1982.

3. Terry Lovell, 'Ideology and Coronation Street' in Richard Dyer et al. (eds.), *Coronation Street,* BFI, London 1981.

4. *RTE Guide,* Jan. 4th, 1980.

5. Charlotte Brunsdon, 'Crossroads: Notes on Soap-Opera', paper to Rutgers University Conference, 'Perspectives on TV and Video Art' 1981.

7 Form, Content and Irish Television*

Kevin Rockett

In a contribution to the discussion on the implications of new video technologies for television programmes about the arts, novelist and presenter/editor of *The South Bank Show,* Melvyn Bragg, observed that "the producer's intentions must group around a narrative clarity".[1] On the following page he reported that a *South Bank Show* poetry competition attracted 35,000 entries and an anthology was produced. Between these two spheres, the producer's perception of the audience's desire for narrativisation and the audience's response to an invitation to participate in the medium lies a central problematic, not the least of which is the notion of the "professional" broadcaster. It is indicative of their perceived role that in the collection of essays in which the article by Bragg is located, *The Third Age of Broadcasting,* a wide group of television and film practitioners contribute to the debate on new video technologies and their implications for programme production without seriously questioning the basis of their own relationship to production: "professionalism" and narrativisation.

As indicated in the Introduction to this volume, the revision of this paper enabled the author to take into consideration the RTE Access Community TV series, screened after the IFI Summer School took place. The paper originally presented at the Summer School concentrated on a British model of 'access' television, the BBC's 'Open Door', but the transmission of RTE's own 'access' television provided a more valuable and immediately relevant focus for the author's analysis. As a development of his arguments published in In Dublin *(see note 14 below) Michael T. Murphy has written his own analysis of the first series, in the form of an RTE internal discussion document –* Access Community Television: a report on the first series 1983/84 by Michael T. Murphy, Producer/Director *(RTE, August 1984) – which discusses the concept, approach, objectives and limitations of the series. This appeared while the present volume was in the press, and Kevin Rockett was therefore unable to take it into account when revising this paper.*

Present Practices

The notion of professionalism carries with it a range of often intimidating meanings for the outsider. It is assumed that there is a set way of making programmes: the professional must ensure that the smooth flow of the television medium will wash over the television watcher. This flow, through the use of conventions or the established patterns of making programmes, is designed to ensure the limitation of doubt or questioning on the part of the audience. Professionalism in this manner really means the maintenance of a homogenous world view that generally corresponds to a reflection of the dominant characteristics of the programme makers: white, male, middle class and heterosexual. It is also a peculiar facet of broadcasters that they do not see themselves as being members of the public, or even of a viewing audience which is being addressed. They are, somehow, a breed apart.

It is through narrative that this homogenous and undisturbing world view is most frequently represented. But narrative is not confined to so-called "drama" productions. Drama productions generally have a fairly obvious story which develops from an initial outline of the characters and their relationships through one or more disruptive events or questions which produce the "drama". By the end the conflicts and contradictions which have been set up during the course of the play or film are resolved. This closes the narrative with a new stability and a new equilibrium is established. Throughout the drama the soundtrack of dialogue, natural sounds and/or music reinforces the veracity of the images shown. This enclosed narrative structure is the basis of most television drama and is rarely departed from. What is, perhaps, more surprising is that a similar structure underlies most television productions.

If we take the "objectification" of the world through news programmes as an example we find that, from the introductory logo, film/photo images and music through to the final item, a recurring structure is evident. The initial images seek to indicate the urgency and global or comprehensive nature of the news. This is underpinned by the news reader usually displaying a distanced, objectified voice. A summary of the main events which are to follow will move from the "heavier" news stories to a concluding "hook" story which will seek to retain the audience through providing a narrative enclosure with an item on sport, a lighthearted event, a "good" news story (or, in the case of Britain, a story about the national unifier and symbol of homogeneity, the Royal Family).

The news items themselves will concentrate on the "dramatic" elements of a story. In fact a *story* is unlikely to make a news programme unless it carries evidence of violence, conflict or disaster. This is most clearly evident in the case of Northern Ireland when an item will be carried only if there is an explosion, a shooting, a death or further political disagreement. It is so rare for British and Irish television news to carry background information, the context of the event, that it is hardly surprising that Irish people are perceived abroad to have an unsatiable and irrat ional attachment to violence and conflict. Similarly in Britain and to a lesser extent in Ireland items on trade union activities become news when there is conflict on a picket line or their action in pursuit of their demands is presented as leading to the company's, community's and their own economic ruin. Disruption and violence are presented as ends in themselves. In this manner understanding structural relationships within the society is either ignored or regulated to the mediation of "neutral" experts. Of course, this view of the world is constructed ideologically to reinforce the safety and security evident in the newsreader's presentation of the final item of narrative closure.

In the case of current affairs which is seen as the in-depth analysis of the "news behind the news," similar narrative strategies are pursued. If we look at two programmes by RTE's main current affairs programme, *Today Tonight,* one on drugs in working class communities, the other an investigation of land speculation, we find that both programmes were marked by the continuous thrust of the television medium towards dramatic conflict — something which was operating quite independent of the programme makers' intentions.

The world of drugs and crime provided material for a series of dramatic encounters and television high points. The reporter confronted members of a criminal family; so-called vigilantes patrolling housing complexes; an ex-drug dealer spoke of criminal violence. These events brought the programme from one dramatic pitch to the next. But the reporter never explained the wider context of the events, or stood aside and downgraded his own mediation of the reality of these people's lives. He did not explain more than the surface conflict which was the material for television drama. It was not surprising, therefore, to hear the response of the residents' groups who felt cheated by the programme makers. They had engaged in dialogue with the programme makers and felt betrayed when drama overwhelmed explanation. In turn the television audience was not offered a useful interpretation of the events or a space in which they could enter with their ideas. The producer of the programme series later dismissed the complaints as bordering on interference in journalistic objectivity or, even worse, censorship. With this type of division between broadcasters and public it is not surprising that the broadcasting institution is perceived as being remote from its various audiences.

The same intrepid reporter put considerable energy and originality into trying to uncover the backers of a massive land speculation project in north County Dublin. This programme had ingredients lacking in the drugs programme: political and economic power in the person of the media's *bete noire,* Charles Haughey, a property developer and an associate of Haughey's and an embattled residents association engaged in a titanic struggle to stop the land re-zoning deal which could ultimately make the land worth hundreds of millions of pounds. With the aid of diagrams, a mass of dates, names and minor characters the complex interconnections of various companies all apparently inexorably leading to a company with known Haughey links was shown. The anti-climatic conclusion showed not surprisingly that Charles Haughey was not at the centre of every land speculation deal in Dublin, even if it remained to be seen whether or not he was involved with this one.

While recognising the links of these various individuals and companies with a particular bank the programme left unexamined the policies of financing such deals. The wider issue of building policy, in particular housing policy, was also ignored. Nowhere in the programme was the audience allowed to register their questions and doubts. This isolated event, one out of hundreds that is in the public domain, was not utilised to develop a wider understanding of land speculation. In short no space was provided in which the audience could articulate their ideas and develop an analytical approach to the situation: the film constructed a world view of the developer and his associates which was so removed from the television viewer that she/he would simply return to her/his isolated viewing experience, unable to engage with the programme at an active level. The viewer was watching what was in effect an *enclosed narrative* about land deals.

I would add one important qualification to this criticism of *Today Tonight* and its RTE2 counterpart *Public Account.* The presentation of often excellently researched programmes on a wide variety of issues, especially about the South's tortuous industrial and social modernisation process has succeeded in focussing attention on issues of urban culture and social class and helped place them on the agenda of Irish political debate. This has provided an important counterpoint to the traditional homogeneity of Irish political culture. It has also served to focus attention specifically on the South and not simply displace, like other elements of Irish society, all its critical energies in pursuit of an island-nation. Despite this qualification however it is necessary to point out that the television forms used to express these radical critiques have themselves often resonated with traditional imagery even in the urban landscape. For example, the planners artificially constructed urban communities have been represented in a manner analogous to that of an integrated rural community with a clear sense of local identity, rather than something with very different histories, problems and possibilities.

Crucial to the thrust of enclosed narrative is the need for the individualisation of characters: success or failure will be determined by the ability of the mythical average viewer to identify with the individual at the centre of the dramatic conflict. This may be a "character" in a play, current affairs programme or the news but it is also true of sport, whether it concerns snooker or soccer — probably the most widely watched sport in Ireland due to *The Big Match* and *Match of the Day* (which is rebroadcast by RTE). These programmes are constructed with an emphasis on the finished product, the goal scored by the star player with the brilliant touch and financial value. The crowd/audience are of interest mainly when there is a riotous disturbance. It is easy to appreciate that there is an ideology at work here: the individualising of the event on the pitch or amongst the players in favour of the lengthy prior process through which a goal becomes a goal. What is effaced is the hard work in gaining fitness, in practice and the building up not just of individual skill but, more importantly, team-work. In short, what is effaced or debased is collective action in favour of individualism.

It is also that same collectivity which is most completely effaced in television and film production in favour of the star billing of a "name" actor, writer or director. Because of the division of labour in film and television production between technicians and "creative" personnel, those who carry out the technical functions are rarely engaged in the development of ideas about what is due to be filmed. It is as if their contribution to a production can only be in following the often conventional aspirations of the director. Whether in deciding on lighting levels, sound mix, photographic style or editing, a series of conventional ways of making a programme have developed and technicians are rarely encouraged to break those moulds. It is possible to appreciate, therefore, the fetish of high technology by technicians who are excluded from the creative process and merely service the conventional aspirations of the director or producer.[2]

But there is a substantial tradition which has sought to find new forms of visual and aural expression and thereby alter the relationship of the film/television text to the audience/viewer.

Alternatives

Firstly, let us take an often ignored aspect of television form, sound. As Mandy Rose has reported "sound recordists and technicians often complain that nobody notices the sound unless it goes wrong".[3] The sound track elements, verbal and non-verbal, are often ignored in critical assessments of films, except when in the case of verbal elements such as dialogue, voiceover and lyrics, are related to the images. As Rose notes, "they are deliberately employed in film and television as inauspicious contributions to the meaning. On another level this is because, with the exception of music, they only make sense in combination with other elements of the soundtrack, or the images".[4] This is true at least with the form of naturalistic and realistic television we have today.

By contrast in their "Statement on Sound Aesthetics" (1926) Eisenstein, Pudovkin and Alexandrov called for non-synchronous sound as a principle of the sound film. They believed that sound/image unity offered by sync. sound was in opposition to their theories of montage which perceived a dialectical relationaship between images and which involved the audience emotionally and intellectually in the production of meaning. Similarly Hans Eisler and Theodor Adorno's *Composing for Films* (1947) criticised the predominant use of music as an aid to instant comprehension in film and called for a musical form which would distance the audience through a process of dialectical interaction. Some experimental film-makers have pursued this course during the past thirty years.

Those who have been concerned with the aesthetics of sound have also been those who have fundamentally examined the basis of film form. The emergence of the filmic avant-garde, with its wide diversity of film-makers, is too broad a topic to pursue here. However, reference can be made to two major strands in the avant-garde which have been identified by Peter Wollen[5] and these then related to the traditional opposition perceived, since cinema began, between drama and documentary in the work of Méliès and the Lumière Brothers.

These two strands originate from different cultural and historical traditions and operate within different institutional and aesthetic practices. On the one hand there is an anti-narrative tradition which operates in opposition to dominant commercial cinema while staying within its institutional parameters. On the other hand there is a tradition which is engaged with a complete rejection of narrative often through the Film Co-Op Movement, based on artisanal production and associated with art galleries.

Godard is the exemplary film-maker of the anti-narrative approach: he has continued to work within commercial cinema but has sought to foreground within his films, especially those made since 1968, the deconstruction of narrative itself. This rejection of the nineteenth century realist literary models upon which commercial cinema is based has led to the introduction of a modernist aesthetic concerned with an exploration of film as film, the relationship of the audience to the screen and the film-maker as constructor. Godard's work constitutes an attempt, in short, both to challenge traditional narrative and to involve the viewer in a more dynamic relationship with the film-text. For the Co-Op Movement the closer affinity to the fine and plastic arts has often led to a thrust towards abstraction with a non-narrative formalist exploration of the materiality of film itself.

While both strains of the avant-garde have often been antagonistic towards each other (and many film-makers do not fit easily into either group) it is possible to discern certain common concerns. Both have been, to use the terminology of the semiotics of language, concerned with an exploration of the traditional primacy of the signified (or content) over the signifier (or form of signification) and have sought to alter or even reverse that relationship itself. Within the ambit of film history where the Méliès-Lumière/drama-documentary dichotomy has held sway recent writers on cinema have been more concerned with emphasising

> "*the importance of film as a production or practice in its own right. For them, and this undermines the very foundations of the Lumière-Méliès division, film does not merely "express" or "represent" but is itself an active process of signification through which meaning is produced . . . And this is so even when a film strives to make this appear not the case, to render its forms and techniques "invisible" ".*[6]

One half-way house between traditional narrative and an extension of television form can be found in the work, both inside and outside television, of Ken Loach, Tony Garnett, Jim Allen and others who have adopted and extended the naturalistic or realistic models of television drama and added documentary elements (or vice versa). This work is too well known to need rehearsing here but what is of interest is that the intense debate which ensued when Loach et al blurred and obscured the distinctions between drama and documentary indicated in a very direct manner the contingent nature of the artificial boundaries of television genres.[7]

The limitations of existing television genres require that the alternative approaches to television production which are available be engaged with. The emphasis on literary models with a naturalist form for drama productions, for example, needs to be altered towards an engagement with a modernist aesthetic where the language of expression is part of the constructed text in its invitation to the audience to "make sense", to participate in the production of meaning, to become even at this basic level producers. An audience equipped, in this manner, with the critical tools could find any programme of interest. The genre separation of news bulletins with their disruptive, violent events, isolated without context, needs to be combined with the issue-based approach of current affairs. Then the individual "story" or issue should resonate with wider meaning as the gap between the news bulletin and the background of current affairs is eliminated.

To achieve a new form of television it will be necessary to involve groups and individuals in a more direct manner in television production. Every day groups and individuals are spoken for by television. They usually have little or no control over how they are represented, as the professional broadcasters and their limited use of the medium confines the mode of representation. Even the medium's mediation between programmes through continuity/presentation and advertising needs to be altered. Continuity/presentation often provides a preferred reading of the programme or film to be screened whether through emphasising stars or director, or warning of a somewhat different programme which might disrupt the smooth flow of television. This signalling of difference is ensured to marginalise or ghettoise innovation. Advertising, like much of the rest of television production, is occupied by predominantly white middle class nuclear families. Sex roles are conventionalised: women cook but do not mend cars; men eat and drink but do not cook, except, perhaps, when the process of cooking is itself ridiculed or hierarchised through the male cook becoming a chef. The social basis of advertising needs to be altered otherwise efforts to change the basis of programmes will be affected by the conceptions of the advertising market. But the social basis of advertising is only one aspect of a wider problematic, the disenfranchisement from television of groups such as the working class or women.

Television's response to this criticism has not been to enfranchise these groups but to provide a veneer of democracy through programmes for discussing television output. While RTE does not have such a programme to discuss its productions the medium has usually presented producer-based programmes in response to this situation such as the BBC's *Did You See . . .?* But even in such a significant exception as Channel Four's *Right of Reply* there is little or no examination of the process of the flow of information to the audience, the nature of the medium itself or of the politics of decision-making in television. There is an absence of discussion of what voices may be heard and those which are spoken for. The rather laughable intervention of the audience, with the exception of *Right of Reply's* Video Box, is through so-called humorous viewer letters such as RTE's *Mailbag* and the BBC's *Points of View*.

But the difficulties of producing an alternative programme series are very easily underestimated. One of the originators of the Independent Film-Makers Association's radical proposals for an innovative Channel Four,[8] John Ellis, was himself given the franchise to produce Channel Four's regular series on Cinema, *Visions.* He candidly detailed the difficult and abrupt transition between critical analysis of institutions and aesthetics and working for one of those institutions. The central problem for Ellis' production company, Large Door, was how to respond to the way in which television traditionally dealt with the arts in general and the cinema in particular (for example Barry Norman's witty but unanalytical Film programme). The question Large Door sought to pose was whether it should treat the *Visions* programmes as the irruption of cinema into TV by using cinematic forms of address. Should it assume viewing attitudes that belong to cinema rather than TV? Amongst other difficulties faced by Large Door was how to break the "narrow band of speech pattern and body language that is acceptable to British TV".[9] This attempt to enfranchise on *Visions* those film critics who had been excluded from television led to concerns about unprofessional presenters (i.e. untrained in television speech etc.). Much of the criticism of the *Visions* programmes hinged on the concept of the audience. But as Ellis points out, the audience "who were adduced are always other people . . . other people who abhor complexity; other people who invariably use TV (even th marginal late-night TV of *Visions: Cinema* slot) as a source of entertainment spiced with information".[10] Ellis also observed that the use of the concept of the "audience", the dependence on statistics, "mark the real isolation of the broadcasters from other viewers".[11]

The Limits of Access

The one attempt to enfranchise that audience into television has been, ironically, to recognise its fragmented and specialised nature. "Access" is often promoted as the solution to the breakdown of the relationship between professional broadcasters and the "audience". However, since it developed on British TV in the early 1970s access has had two restrictions which have allowed an inordinate degree of power to remain in the hands of the broadcasters, even in the so-called access slot. Firstly, there is the selection of groups or individuals who may make programmes (which may be termed an internal political issue unless the selection procedure is democratised). Secondly, and more importantly, there is a problem concerning the availability of equipment and the knowledge of the skills to use it. Broadcast video skills are confined to the broadcasting institution while film skills are more widely available outside television. But even with the BBC's *Open Door* film was available only to one group in six and then at a shooting rate of 3 to 1 compared with the normal 10 to 1 ratio. But it is the process of learning the limits and possibilities of the medium itself, and how a finished programme should be constructed, which has created the most difficulty for access users. Even with the resolution of this issue through the making of a satisfactory programme, the programme policy of the broadcasting institution intervenes to place the programme in a time and place in the programme schedule over which the makers have no power. The television guide and continuity announcer signal the particular difference of the access programme to the audience. Thus the most serious issue of all for the temporarily enfranchised programme maker, ghettoisation of experimentation and innovation, will isolate or reduce the value of the access slots. This ghettoisation of the access slots will have served merely to reinforce the professional, smooth flow of other television programmes.

The BBC's *Open Door*, which began broadcasting in 1973, provides evidence of the dilemma presented to outsiders who wish to be accepted to make a programme or, when accepted, who must go about making a programme. In one year six hundred groups or individuals applied for forty programme slots. The selection, according to the programme series producer, was "a fearful burden on time and mind. The process made the election of a Pope look simple and was far too cumbersome to be described here".[12] If ever there existed a broadcaster's cop-out this is it! However, there does exist a detailed account of the experience of one group who made a programme for *Open Door*. This programme, *It Ain't Half Racist, Mum*, on racism on British television, could be described as being more overtly political than other access programmes in the sense that it sought to explore underlying structural racism in British society and how this was manifest in television. Most other access programmes have tended to deal with isolated groups concerned with poverty, deprivation or unusual social activities, and make little or no attempt to relate the specific issue to the general social context. In the case of *It Ain't Half Racist, Mum,* which was made by people some of whom had an understanding of the limits and possibilities of the medium and others who had worked professionally in television, the concern was with issues of representation and television aesthetics. It was the first programme devoted to a critical look at the medium itself and this proved to be one of its problems as ITN and BBC News refused to provide material for the programme. Later two of BBC's current affairs "super-stars", Robin Day and Ludovic Kennedy, received an apology from the BBC after threatening to sue for what they perceived as an attempt in the programme to accuse them of racism.

What proved most difficult for the group was how to find and use a form of representation which broke established moulds and expressed the group's analysis of racism in the medium. Some of the group sought an irruption of the medium's smooth flow which could be part of the programme structure. However, every time some innovative idea was suggested the limits of the medium, the availability of time, or more crucially, the response of the professional television people in the group would ensure that their perceived need to make the programme "comprehensible" and thus adopt conventional forms would override considerations of formal innovation. One of the group's members later noted how the television professionals unconsciously incorporated television conventions into their assessment of the programme's radical content:

> "... the skills and values of "professionalism" were regarded as neutral and useful resources, not as the particular outcome of a process of ideological and institutional formation within the television companies. It seemed to us that the group's programme makers had in this formative training "internalised" a fairly orthodox television aesthetic which they were not prepared to question and which contradicted their other politics. It was the members of the group who had not worked directly in television production who argued for taking risks in the style and content of the programme. We wanted the programme to be **offensive**, to look different as well as to encompass different political ideas. We did not see the two as separate . . ."[13]

If the procedures of production are regarded as neutral then the question needs to be posed to broadcasters on what grounds can choices be made as to when to use a close up, a long shot, a pan or a zoom. These are not just technical details but decisions which will help determine the meaning of the programme. For example, an interview is usually shot with both interviewer and interviewee, then a displacement of the audience's medium shot and wide shot. But if a pan was used back and forth between the two, or even to something outside the space of the interviewer and interviewee, then a displacement of the audience's expectation could service to focus on what is said rather than on the individual who says it. It would also serve to remind the audience that this interview is itself an artificial construction. An offensive programme with a disruptive visual style would encourage people to stop and think, to become distanced from the medium's smooth flow.

RTE's one notable experiment in access until the recent past, *It's a Hard Oul' Station* (1976), disrupted the flow of television even at the basic level of using a working class woman's voice to explain not just the underlying issues of unemployment and deprivation within her Dublin inner city community but to relate these problems to a wider social sphere where the policies of the Industrial Development Authority and politicians were shown to be inadequate. The programme's final disruption of the viewing space sought not to enclose the programme with a smooth ending but used the image of a car bomb explosion in Belfast with a voice over indicating that maybe the next time you, the television audience, hear of such an event it may be expressing the anger and frustration of Irish workers.

By contrast with this angry irruption of television through a temporary enfranchisement of a normally excluded voice lies the formal blandness of an RTE series entitled *Access Community Television* broadcast from November 1983 until April 1984. Most of the programmes on subjects as diverse as young travellers in Galway, young music students and young Garda recruits, conformed to a television form which could have as easily fitted into any television slot without the use of the code words "access" and "community". One of these programmes, on access to schools for the disabled, raised a minor controversy in *In Dublin* when that magazine's writer on television, Lelia Doolan, an experienced ex-RTE producer and a committed advocate of decentralised community television, questioned the mediation of both the professional broadcaster and the medium itself. Throughout the series the programme presenter, Ciana Campbell, often quite skilfully, succeeded in getting individuals and groups to explain their world view. The quality of her mediation through a relaxed interview style elicited views and attitudes not normally presented on RTE. However, this is a rather different matter than the groups themselves questioning the whole basis of their relationship to the medium and finding a form through which their ideas could be presented. While some groups used drama inserts or invited the viewing audience to write to them for further information about their activities it is indicative of the institutionalised approach to access that even an obviously sympathetic series producer would mystify television programme making by observing that access groups "have neither the time nor the inclination to assemble the cameras, work them, haul cables, nor indeed set up lamps nor position

143

the various types of microphone, learn the technicalities of how an editing machine works, etc.".[14] It is possible to make a formally innovative programme given time and willingness on the part of the institution without having to become an apprentice or a film school student as the writer of the above I'm sure knows quite well.

One of the notable exceptions in the series which tried to confront directly the medium itself and their representation on it was made by members of the Dublin Gay Federation. (Another innovative programme was made by Dublin's Grapevine Arts Centre). From the opening image of a pan across ordinary city terraced houses a discussion by young gay people immediately posed the question as to how it is possible to communicate the experience of gay people on television and then cram it into twenty-five minutes. Even the question of who the programme was addressing — other gays, straights or both — was raised. But the formal fragmentation of the initial group follows through separate interviews with a lesbian, Scottie, and a gay man. Despite her formal isolation in the interview Scottie raised the issue that even to make a programme on gays was to reinforce their difference rather than their normality. Then in a "Confrontation" highlighted by a title, as were the two interviews, straights expressed their ignorance and prejudice towards gays. This was followed by a lesbian and a gay man being queried by the group and then, when the two had left, the group discussed their attitudes. This section had the unintentional appearance of a crude laboratory experiment when the two bacteria could somehow be enclosed in the straight group. Through dialogue or even confrontation prejudicial attitudes to gays might be overcome. This issue was developed further when a section, "The Mothers", showed two women's difficulties in coming to terms with their children being gay. What was absent and only alluded to in passing was the role of the father within the family, sexual stereotyping in the society in general, and a more developed historical sense of homosexuality. The programme came full circle towards the end when the question was again posed as to whether the programme was worth doing: "Should we have said to RTE that they couldn't possibly make a programme about our lives, whatever you do?". The reply was that RTE couldn't but "twenty-five minutes is something versus nothing". A gay song sung in Dublin's gay Hirschfeld Centre enclosed the narrative and closed the programme.

In a unique departure from television's normal defensive response to criticism the makers of the seventeen *Access Community Television* programmes were invited to discuss their experience in making the programmes and their preception of RTE and television in general. This hour-long programme is as interesting in its formal organisation as is the discussion itself.

Set in a relaxed pub lounge environment the programme-makers were seated in a *dis*-organised manner around the room while Ciana Campbell literally controlled the floor. She stood or walked around the centre of the room dominating the visual space. She selected or invited people to speak as well as identified some of the discussion topics. In addition, she introduced the programme in a jokey manner, an approach which was later underpinned by an insert which purported to explain how a television programme is made. Using still photographs of the making of one of the programmes about farming these were assembled in a photographic narrative with appropriate information and jokey voice-over by Ciana Campbell. This section, with its mystificatory emphasis on cables, lights, cameras, etc., has also a few references to formal decision-making by technicians and the producer. A microphone is put on a "fish-pole" "to pick up the sound without being seen". A lighting director "decided" how he's going to light a scene. A cameraman wants to move to a low-angle to get a "particularly good shot" but the producer asks him to go higher. What, one could ask, is a "good shot", why is low-angle as opposed to a high-angle shot used? The narrativisation concludes when a photograph reveals a dog being restrained while an interview is being filmed. It is all, as Ciana Campbell says in her introduction, a bit unpredictable. The behaviour of the dog may be unpredictable but the behaviour of the technicians hardly is.

Because of the layout of the people during the lounge discussion microphones periodically introduce into wide shot visual space but as soon as a close up of the person speaking can be put in frame on another camera there is an immediate cut to that person. On location the microphone can be carefully excluded from the shot but in the discussion the procedures of production, in this case microphones, are hurriedly effaced from the image if at all possible.

The programme itself has a double enclosure. With further jokey film Ciana Campbell is seen being filmed for a "noddy" or the false or constructed shot regularly used in television interviews. In this instance the person being interviewed is unaware of what a "noddy" is and continues to speak not knowing he may remain silent. Meanwhile Ms. Campbell tries not to laugh. This item ends and the humour is enjoyed with the interviewee becoming aware of his ignorance of what a "noddy" is. Thus the technical ignorance of the lay person reinforces the need for professionals or "experts" who know about such things.

The programme ends with a solemn introduction to two examples of extreme emotional trauma from the series being re-shown. One is an extract from the gay programme when one of the mothers tells of her response to her son telling her that he is gay. The other concerned the response by two members of Coolmine Drug Rehabilitation Centre to being told that they may re-enter the outside world. One of these men, in front of a large number of other residents and the television crew, begins to cry. Thus this programme and the series ends with the direct emotional experience of two traumatic events. Perhaps, the programme producers would suggest, only with community involvement with television can genuine emotional experience be represented.

This was one of the themes taken up in the discussion proper. One contributor observed that programmes which dealt with personal problems could be very political while another, Scottie, from the gay programme, noted the distance between what she had felt and how it appeared. She wanted to express her anger about the need even to make a programme about gay people but found that she came across as a polite person. She noted the need for outside programme-makers to learn the language of television, to acquire the language, as another observed, in a manner analogous to acquiring literacy. Scottie argued for the need to have more time to develop ideas, more contact with the crew and, a recurring topic of discussion, the elimination of the presenter's mediation. Others added that there was a need for continual access to RTE by outside groups and that this should be available as a right and not as a privilege. It is, after all, the national broadcasting system.

The need for "experts", advocated by some, was dismissed by many others and though the issue of what precise division of labour could be envisaged was raised, it was, unsurprisingly, left unresolved. Others expressed an awareness of the cost of making such a programme with a crew of twenty-two and full outside broadcast unit facilities. Some, though, noted that this need not be the only route followed by access users. (All the programmes, incidently, were made with an Outside Broadcast Unit.) One of the final points made was by Scottie who raised an issue central to the argument of this paper. She urged the need to present everything differently. It was necessary to 'subvert the medium' rather than retain a standard form.

I hope it has been established by now that it is not enough to simply allow new or disenfranchised voices to appear on television and expect that the reality of their lives will be presented. It is necessary to involve people directly in the production process, to demystify the technology and actively to explore new forms of expression. From what direction will these innovations come? The existing structure or decision-making needs to be radically overhauled. A concern for the social basis and formal expression of television production must replace the maintenance of a narrow based television consensus. Looking outside television to the Irish independent film-making sector there are some people whose work indicates new exploratory possibilities. But while the independents often regard anything they have produced as being more innovative than an RTE product the fact remains that there are few films from this sector which are formally innovative or have a radically different content. The independents can quite rightly complain that funds are not available for these types of films. RTE, therefore, has the opportunity to set out consciously to produce experimental material, like many European television stations. We need to shift away from our traditional television models, BBC and ITV, towards a more innovative European television service such as RAI in Italy and ZDF in Germany.

REFERENCES

1. "Open Space for Arts" in Brian Wenham, (ed.), *The Third Age of Broadcasting* (London: Faber and Faber, 1982), p. 45.

2. In reference to technology it needs to be pointed out in passing that a certain image quality is maintained by television. The use of lower grade tape would allow, amongst other developments, access to television by non-professionals and independent producers. Perhaps this could be one of the issues in the developing debate concerning new cable channels, though the danger of ghettoising experimentation must be avoided.

3. 'Heard Any Good Programmes Lately?' in Simon Blanchard, David Morley (eds.), *What's This Channel Four?* (London: Comedia, 1982), p. 136. The evidence on alternative sound strategies is taken from this article.

4. Ibid.

5. 'The Two Avant-Gardes', *Studio International*, November/December 1975. Reprinted *Edinburgh '76 Magazine*, No. 1, 1976.

6. John Hill, 'Reel to Real', *Film Directions*, Vol. 3, No. 11, 1980, p. 18.

7. For the details of this debate see Colin McCabe, 'Realism and the Cinema: Notes on Some Brechtian Theses', *Screen*, Vol. 15, No. 2, Summer 1974; Colin MacArthur, 'Days of Hope', *Screen*, Vol. 16, No. 4, Winter 1975/76. See also the above article by John Hill for the wider context of the debate and Christopher Williams (ed.), *Realism and the Cinema* (London: Routledge and Kegan Paul, 1980) for a comprehensive historical account.

8. See 'The Independent Film-makers' Association and the Fourth Channel', *Screen*, Vol. 21, No. 4, 1980/81, pp. 56-79. Some of the ideas on innovation in television are taken from the first of these two articles.

9. John Ellis, 'Channel Four: Working Notes', *Screen*, Vol. 24, No. 6, November/December 1983.

10. Ibid. pp. 50-51.

11. Ibid. p. 51.

12. Paul Bonner, 'Paperback Television', *The Third Age of Broadcasting*, op. cit., p. 100.

13. Carl Gardiner (in collaboration with Margaret Henry), 'Racism, Anti-Russian and Access Television: The Making of *Open Door*', *Screen Education*, No. 31, Summer 1979, p. 74.

14. Michael T. Murphy, 'Trained to Serve', *In Dublin*, No. 196, 26 January 1984, p. 52. Lelia Doolan's article, 'Handicapped Access', was in *In Dublin*, No. 195, 12 January 1984. See also Lelia Doolan, 'Access Makes the Heart Grow Fonder', *In Dublin*, No. 201, 5 April 1984, pp. 46-47.

Appendix 1

De Valera's Address on the opening of Telefís Éireann — 31 December 1961

Báil ó Dia oraibh a uaisil na nGael. Guim sein agus sonas orm san athbliain agus toradh céadtha ar mo cuid oibre. Is mór agam gur mise an céad duine atá labhairt libh ar an seirbís nua seo Telefís Éireann. Tá súil orm go mbainfeadh sibh siamsa agus aoibhneas as, agus comh maith le sin eolas-teagaisc agus eolas. Ní raibh go dtí seo i lámh an duine aon sort cumhacht. Tá dóchas agam go neireoigh linne í a chur chun tairbhre cóir.

As I said I am privileged in being the first to address you on our new service Telefís Éireann. I hope the service will provide for you all sources of recreation and pleasure but also information, instruction and knowledge. I must admit that sometimes when I think of television and radio and their immense power, I feel somewhat afraid. Like atomic energy it can be used for incalculable good but it can also do irreparable harm. Never before was there in the hands of men an instrument so powerful to influence the thoughts and actions of the multitude. The persistent policy pursued over radio and television, apart from imparting knowledge can build up the character of the whole people inducing sturdiness and vigour and confidence. On the other hand, it can lead through demoralization to decadence and disillusion. Sometimes one hears, when one urges higher standards in information and recreation services, that one must give the people what they want. And the competition unfortunately is in the wrong direction so standards become lower and lower.

Now it is you the people who will ultimately determine what the programmes in Telefís Éireann are to be. If you insist on having presented to you the good the true and the beautiful you will get this and I for one will find it hard to be convinced that good taste can not be cultivated. I find it hard to believe for example that a person who views the grandeurs of the heavens, or the wonders of this marvelous mysterious world in which the good God has placed us will not find more pleasure in that than in viewing for example some squalid domestic brawl or a street quarrel. I feel sure that full use will be made of the immense repertory which is now at our disposal. Apart altogether from the wonders of nature we have the great achievements of man himself — the masterpieces of architecture, engineering, sculpture, painting. And who, on looking at those or hearing the great musical compositions of the great composers would want to descend to anything lower. I have great hopes in this new service. I am confident that those who are in charge will do everything in their power to make it useful for the nation, that they will bear in mind that we are an old nation and that we have our own distinctive characteristics and that it is desirable that these be preserved. I am sure that they will do their part and as I have said it is for the public now to do theirs.

I wish all those who are in charge God speed and I wish all of you a very happy New Year. Beannacht Dé agaibh agus cuimirce ó Mhuire ar an náisiún ársa na nGael.

Appendix 2

TABLE 1

Urban/Rural Analysis of Audience

| | | Total Households | | Household with RTE1 | | | Household with RTE2 | |
		000's	%	%	000's	%	000's	%
1963	Urban	269	(40)	100	136	51		
	Rural	408	(60)	100	101	25		
1966	Urban	302	(44)	100	236	78		
	Rural	388	(56)	100	144	37		
1971	Urban	350	(49)	100	310	89		
	Rural	355	(51)	100	226	64		
1976	Urban	435	(55)	100	394	91		
	Rural	351	(45)	100	261	74		
1981	Urban	486	(54)	100	467	96	438	90
	Rural	414	(46)	100	358	87	317	77
1983	Urban	512	55		483	94	469	92
	Rural	415	45		360	87	340	82

TABLE 2

Proportion of Single and multi channel homes

Year	Total Homes (estimates) 000's	Total TV Homes 000's	%	Single Channel 000's	%	Multi Channel 000's	%
1963	667	237	100	123	52	114	48
1966	690	380	100	239	63	141	37
1971	705	536	100	336	63	200	37
1976	786	655	100	367	56	288	44
1981	900	825	100	430	52	395	48
1983	927	843	100	435	51	408	49

TABLE 3

Number of Hours Broadcast

Year	Total Hours		Home Produced		Imported	
	Hours	%	Hours	%	Hours	%
1962	562	100	275	49	286	51
1966	2,297	100	1,182	51	1,115	49
1971	2,360	100	1,049	44	1,311	56
1976	3,196	100	1,304	41	1,892	59
1980	5,818	100	1,883	32	3,935	68
1980 RTE1	3,631	100	1,412	39	2,218	61
1980 RTE2	2,186	100	470	22	1,716	72